A MACAO NARRATIVE

D1713400

Echoes: Classics of
Hong Kong Culture and History

The life of Hong Kong has been described and explored in many books, literary, historical and scholarly. The purpose of *Echoes* is to make the best of those books available and accessible in order to bring their insights and reading pleasure to a new and wider readership.

———————————

Other titles in the Echoes series:

Power and Charity: A Chinese Merchant Elite in Colonial Hong Kong
  Elizabeth Sinn

A Biographical Sketch-book of Early Hong Kong
  G. B. Endacott

Chinese Christians: Elites, Middlemen and the Church in Hong Kong
  Carl T. Smith

Edge of Empires: Chinese Elites and British Colonials in Hong Kong
  John M. Carroll

Anglo-China: Chinese People and British Rule in Hong Kong, 1841–1880
  Christopher Munn

City of Broken Promises
  Austin Coates

Macao and the British, 1937–1842: Prelude to Hong Kong
  Austin Coates

The Road
  Austin Coates

A MACAO NARRATIVE

Austin Coates

With a Foreword by
César Guillén Nuñez

香港大學出版社

Hong Kong University Press

Hong Kong University Press
14/F Hing Wai Centre
7 Tin Wan Praya Rd
Aberdeen
Hong Kong

© Austin Coates 1978, 2009

First published by Heinemann Educational Book (Asia) Ltd. in 1978
This edition published by Hong Kong University Press in 2009

ISBN 978-962-209-077-4

Secure on-line Ordering
www.hkupress.org

Printed and bound by Pre-Press Ltd., Hong Kong, China

Foreword

When Austin Coates' *A Macao Narrative* was first published in 1978, Western historians of his generation had to contend with a literature not yet fully developed, in which parts of the city's history had been fictionalized. Brave attempts at writing a history of Macao had been made previously. There was Sir Andrew Ljungstedt's *An Historical Sketch of the Portuguese Settlements in China*, written in English and published in Boston in 1836 by James Munroe & Co., but partly written in Macao in 1832. In spite of its misleading title—the book is really a history of the city, with an additional chapter on Canton—this was the first attempt at a modern, more sober interpretation of facts regarding the founding and subsequent history of Macao. As it clashed with mythical accounts it was not fully accepted by the Portuguese. Then, for the first time in the city's history a textbook claiming to present the main facts of the territory's history was published with the title *Resumo da História de Macau*. It was written several years before its publication in 1927, by the French cleric Regis Gervaix, using the *nom de plume* Eudore de Colomban. But neither text could match the large volume by Montalto de Jesus' *Historic Macao*, published in 1902, but significantly revised in its 1926 edition. A use of outmoded English by the Portuguese-speaking Macanese historian sometimes obscured the passionate author's ideas, while his strong nationalism tended to lead him, in certain passages, back to a Macao of folk tales. *A Macao Narrative* is quite different from these seminal works, and was equally a first of its kind.

In his narrative Austin Coates aimed to provide a simple, uncontroversial recounting of the city's history. Easy and enjoyable to read, *A Macao Narrative* was not conceived for academic purposes, but rather for an intelligent reader who might wish to learn the most important aspects of Macao's history. A first-time reader might well be carried away by the easy flow of the prose, the witty remarks, the elegance of the author's style—an elegance he had inherited from his patrician upbringing under his father, the composer Eric Coates. The ease with which Austin Coates recounted even the most dramatic events, as if holding a lively conversation, demonstrates that his narrative is, in fact, an exceptional history of the city. This facility for turning complicated and confused events into a fascinating story should not blind us to his integrity as a historian. To cite but two examples, his discerning choice and consideration of complex events are shown in his narration of Ljungstedt's role in bringing to the fore unpalatable facts about Macao's foundation, or in his chronicle of the less explainable reasons for Vicente Nicolau de Mesquita's victory at Pak Shan Han against superior Chinese forces. As regards the Chinese, not only his intellectual integrity but also his innate sense of fair play did not let him diminish their important intervention in shaping the enclave's history.

Although Austin Coates' account may not yield to mythic interpretations, his genuine affection for Portuguese culture does at times emerge in this book as a kind of homage. His somewhat romantic approach is evident from the very opening lines of the preface, where he writes that upon waking he tends to associate Macao with Venice. This statement will certainly cause many a raised eyebrow if it were to be understood in an art-historical or cultural sense. Macao has certainly never matched the artistic legacy of Venice, a fact of which at least a number of Portuguese themselves, who created Macao, were well aware. Manuel da Silva Mendes, for instance, writing in 1929 for the newspaper *Jornal de Macau*, in which he gave a positive appraisal of the city's already vanishing cultural heritage, wonderfully expressed it: *Eu bem sei que Macau nunca foi uma Florença* (I only know too well that Macao was never Florence). Silva Mendes had seen Macao just before its twentieth-century modernization, but he realized that there was no need to turn it into a legend, or an Orient-that-never-was of the Romantics or the Orientalists. To be sure, the city has

vi

its own charm, its own style, but it is that of a Portuguese colonial city and a Southern Chinese village, where the Chinese and Portuguese begat a unique cultural environment.

The epistemological preoccupations of present-day historians may provide more balanced, dispassionate historical accounts. They usually incorporate modern methods of enquiry and try to evaluate different sides of the same question. While this is evidently the best, perhaps the only way, to get closer to historical truth, there may be a danger of losing the dramatic highlights of previous histories. In this sense Austin Coates' approach to history is closer to traditional narrative and appears immune from the multifaceted and multi-voiced discourse of postmodernism. The author manages to keep focused, to keep a sense of the greatness of the Portuguese achievements in the Far East and of Macao's significance in this enterprise, no matter how censurable the more negative effects of Western colonization. In fact, the first significant meeting of East and West of modern times was first made possible by a deliberate act on the part of a small European kingdom enjoying a cultural flowering, in part due to the impact of the Italian Renaissance. As reader we are left to marvel at this achievement.

Austin Coates and the generation of scholars and writers to which he belonged were pioneers in the field—those quoted in his select bibliography are amongst the best examples, even if they did not all produce unified histories of the city. It may not be too extravagant to liken them to the Portuguese explorers, in the sense that they opened up new routes for the intellect in charting a more exact history of Portuguese discoveries and of Macao's role in it. In doing so, they also helped us see Macao in its true perspective and not only as the gambling capital for which it is almost exclusively known to most today.

More Vegas than Venice, Macao has been transformed beyond belief in the three decades since the book was first published. At the time that Austin Coates was writing gambling was already a main attraction, but Macao still retained the air of a provincial

Portuguese town with all the time in the world. A taxi or two might pass by the city's main restaurants in the Praia Grande, which was still partly intact. The famous Praia was often before the author's eyes from the balcony of his favourite hotel rooms at the old Bela Vista. It may have been there that the mirage of Venice first appeared to this somewhat eccentric, cigar-smoking, Edwardian gentleman.

Soon after the publication of *A Macao Narrative* the city began its last chapter as a Portuguese settlement. Following the grand projects of redevelopment devised by one of the last Portuguese governors of the enclave, there have been extensive reclamations in the Outer Harbour and the adjoining islands of Taipa and Coloanne, and the Praia is gone. The status of the city as a gambling centre of the region has soared, with revenues that surpass Las Vegas. Ironically perhaps, Venice has materialized in the form of The Venetian, the biggest casino in the world, complete with gondolas, St. Mark's Square and a Bridge of Sighs.

Soon before Macao's return to China corruption and crime appeared like circling vultures. But so did a renewed interest in the city's culture and history. A turning point took place on the stroke of midnight on 19 December 1999, as the Chinese flag rose and the Portuguese national flag was lowered during the handover ceremony. A new Macao came into being; following the Basic Law, it became the Special Administrative Region of Macao, with an independent Chief Executive chosen from the local population. Macao's very name now is, more often than not, *Ou-Mun*, the Chinese name for the peninsula. As it returned to the mother country, a Portuguese Consul General moved into the Bela Vista Hotel above Bom Parto Fort, which became his private residence. Austin Coates' Macao will slowly fade from view, although the city's history, as seen through his eyes, will not easily fade from memory.

César Guillén Nuñez
2009

"Not even the celebrated Rialto, at Venice, transacted a volume of trade exceeding that which was carried on at Macao. Here, in Macao, men of two continents met and had discourse, in peace, even when no other spot could be found for the purpose in the Farthest East."

J. M. BRAGA
The Western Pioneers and Their Discovery of Macao

Acknowledgments

I would like to acknowledge the debt I owe to four personal friends: to the historian J. M. Braga, in San Francisco, for originally suggesting that I take up this subject, and for his comments and criticisms; to the photographer Christiane Pikert Scharlau, in Hamburg, for graciously allowing me to reproduce her pictures, some of which she took specially for this book; and in Macao itself, to the architect Jorge Graça for making available to me, from his own private collection, copies of the splendid 18th-century Chinese maps, two of which appear as illustrations, the third as the back endpaper;* and to the historian Father Manuel Teixeira for helping to clarify a number of obscure points, and for his general encouragement at all times.

* *Publisher's Note:* The illustrations to which the author refers, which appeared in earlier editions of the book, have not been reproduced in the present edition.

Preface

I always associate Macao with Venice. Whichever one I am in, I always wake up wondering which one it is.

It has nothing to do with canals. Macao has none.

It is due to the condition that both were once among the greatest trading centres in the world, tightly confined to a minute segment of land surrounded by water, yet not quite an island.

The difference is that Macao never had a Bridge of Sighs. There were no dungeons. Nor did the Inquisition ever come there.

How Macao was founded is to me fascinating. In conveying the story now—and, I hope, some of the fascinations—I propose to begin at the beginning, as all stories should. The reader who wishes to plunge straight into Macao may begin at Chapter 3.

The story begins on the heights of the Ponta de Sagres, one of the southernmost points in Portugal, not far from Cape St Vincent. Standing on the heights of Sagres is similar to being on top of Beachy Head, save that it is much grander, and beneath it is that sound, the Atlantic Ocean which is not so much a roar as a message.

Upon that height, long ago, a prince stood in solitude, heard that message, and interpreted it.

A.C.
Hongkong
1977

Contents

Foreword, by César Guillén Nuñez   v

Acknowledgments   x

Preface   xi

1   Portuguese Asia: Why and How   1

2   Squatters on the China Coast   17

3   The Golden Age of the Japan Trade   31

4   Dutch Assaults on Macao   53

5   The Passing of Macao's Golden Epoch   63

6   Outpost of all Europe   81

7   Sovereignty   110

Bibliography   141

Index   144

1
Portuguese Asia: Why and How

Discovery of the sea route to India

Portugal's stupendous epoch of exploration and discovery began around 1419, when the first Portuguese reached the island of Porto Santo in the Madeira group following this in 1420 with the discovery of Madeira itself. The initiator of the Discoveries, a person in some ways so strikingly modern and different from his age that he seems to belong more to the twentieth century than to the fifteenth, was the Infante Dom Henrique—Prince Henry the Navigator—the austere, unemotional third son of João I of Portugal and his English queen Philippa, daughter of John of Gaunt. On the heights of Sagres Prince Henry conceived the then incredible idea of making the ocean, beyond which it was believed lay nothingness, into a highway by means of which to reach other lands.

Without himself ever travelling further than Tangier, Prince Henry listened to sea-captains' experiences, examined old travellers' tales and traditions, and after a thorough study of all that in those days could be learnt of geography and navigation, including Arab knowledge which was then the most advanced, he organized from his retreat near the port of Lagos in southern Portugal a series of exploratory voyages down the west coast of Africa. His motives were, like the man himself, a compelling mixture of medieval and modern: to examine the nature of lands hitherto unknown to Europeans, to seek new avenues of trade, to find out how far the dominion of Islam extended, to learn whether there were possibly some unknown Christian kingdoms willing to join in war against Islam, and finally to bring the Christian faith to any willing to receive it.

Europe was threatened, almost encircled by Islam. The entire east and south coasts of the Mediterranean, from Turkey to Morocco, were occupied by a hostile belt of Islamic states; and although the conquering energy of the Arabs had spent itself, the Turks had taken up the faltering banner of the Crescent. In 1453 they captured Constantinople, thereby extinguishing the Eastern Roman Empire, considered to be Christian Europe's main eastern bulwark against Islam. The salvation of Europe from this menace was the foremost military and political problem of the age.

Another lesser problem was associated with it. The Crusades, reviving between Europe and the Middle East contacts that had been lost since the heyday of the Roman Empire, had stimulated European demand for a number of oriental products. Of these the most important were pepper and other food seasonings, such as nutmeg, cloves, and cinnamon. Other items were sugar and luxury goods—precious stones, fine silks, cottons, and embroideries. These, brought by sea from different parts of Asia to Baghdad, Damascus, and Alexandria, were transported by caravan across the deserts of the Middle East, then shipped from Egypt and the Levant to Europe's two most important ports, Venice and Genoa, both of which owed their commercial prosperity to what pious Christians considered a disgraceful trade with the infidel. Such was the anomalous situation the Crusades produced. In order to obtain the oriental goods she required, Europe was obliged and willing to buy at exorbitant prices from Islam, her deadly enemy, who was the sole intermediary between West and East.

Maritime exploration, therefore, could lead to two important results, one military and religious, the other commercial—the discovery of a route by which to attack Islam from the rear, and the establishment of direct contact between Europe and the Spice Islands.

This was religion and trade going hand in hand; and as long as activity was confined to the Islamic zone of Asia—the Middle East and the countries bordering the Arabian Sea—the duality of purpose was a natural one. It was only when, sailing still further, Christians came in contact with Hindus, Chinese, and Japanese that the religious design became more complex, changing from a simple crusading determination to stamp out Islam into a dream of establishing a universal Christian state. The change was unavoidable. The Portuguese Discoveries amazed and excited all Europe, and while laymen dreamed of the fortunes they might make in the Indies, it was natural that the leaders of the Christian Church should interpret these developments as a way leading to universal Christianity.

Prince Henry the Navigator died in 1460, when Portuguese vessels were not even halfway down the west coast of Africa, but his work was carried on by others. In the next decades the Gold and Ivory Coasts were reached, and in 1488 Bartolomeu Dias, hugging the coast of Africa in uncertain weather, found himself heading north but with land still to port. He had discovered the Cape of Good Hope.

This was the climax of the first, most dangerous and difficult phase of the Discoveries. Once down the long and inhospitable West African coast and round the Cape of Good Hope, the adventurers entered a region of organized Arab trade and more regular winds and seasons, where at every port there was accurate information to be had concerning other ports, weather conditions, and courses. By taking advantage of such assistance, and with a pilot provided by a friendly East African sultan, Vasco da Gama in 1498 completed the next great phase, and reached the west coast of India. He was now in the heartland of oriental commerce and in the rear of Islam, with a sea route which, if developed, could break Islam's commercial hold on Europe.

3

It remained to secure his tremendous find. Trade in Eastern seas was dangerous for Christians, Mussulman rulers were established throughout Upper India, their power extending gradually southwards, while in the Indies—the principal goal of the spice trade—Arab and Indian Muslim traders and missionaries had succeeded in converting many formerly Hindu or Buddhist states to Islam. None of the Eastern peoples being particularly interested in overseas connexions at this time, Arabs and Gujerati Muslims had monopolized the entire carrying trade of South Asia, with the inestimable advantage of dealing at almost every port with their co-religionists. The Portuguese discovered that the power of Islam was not, as had been originally supposed, a band of influence lying between Christian Europe and Asiatic lands. Islam reached to the furthest ends of the Indies.

It should be borne in mind that up to this time there was still no idea of founding European colonies. But the Portuguese had to protect their lines of operation. They thus constructed what shortly became a chain of fortresses across Asia, carefully disposed at converging points of trade, not too far distant one from another, combining the services of markets, warehouses, barracks, and shipyards. Improving and enlarging their ships, which were then and for another 100 years the most up-to-date in the world, they reckoned that with well-armed trading vessels operating on the routes designated and protected by their coastal forts, they could gain the mastery of the Indian Ocean's trade, and be strong enough to defend it.

The first of the forts was built in 1503 at Cochin, on the south-west coast of India, and was followed by others along the same coast. In 1505 a start was made in East Africa, where within three years there were establishments at Mombasa, Zanzibar, and Moçambique. Finally, approaching the narrowest points on the spice trade's two main routes, they installed themselves on the bare, torrid island of Socotra, dominating the southern entrance to the Red Sea, and in 1509 seized Ormuz at the mouth of the Persian Gulf. By these moves, Alexandria and Baghdad were threatened with the drying-up of supplies from the East.

The Islamic world quickly became aware of the threat this presented to their interests. In 1509 they assembled a tremendous international Muslim fleet, which met the Portuguese under their first Viceroy in the East, Dom Francisco de Almeida, off the west coast of India, near Diu. In a well-matched fight, one of the most significant naval battles in history, the Muslims were routed. Although for many years afterwards the Portuguese still had to contend with Mohammedan naval rivalry, their adversaries were never again able to assemble such power against them. By the Battle of Diu, control of trade between Europe and the East passed from Muslim to Christian hands.

Goa

Celebrating their victory, the Portuguese sailed southward down the Malabar coast, pausing off each Muslim settlement to cannon into its streets one or two limbs of their Muslim prisoners. This uninhibited display was in keeping with the times, the standards of Europe and Asia in matters of this kind being identical.

The following year they seized the port of Goa, a former Hindu city recently absorbed by the Muslims, and transformed it into a tropical headquarters. Forts, churches, colleges, and seminaries were erected with remarkable speed, Goa becoming the capital of the Portuguese mercantile empire, the seat of the Viceroy commanding it, and in addition, the most representative centre of European culture there has ever been in Asia.

A few weeks after Goa's capture, Almeida was succeeded as Viceroy by Afonso de Albuquerque, in some ways the most significant and commanding figure in the history of Portuguese Asia, the nature of which, as a result of his ideas, took a new form, closer to what might be described as colonial. Albuquerque foresaw that with the terrible losses of men by shipwreck, piracy, disease, and warfare, Portugal would not be able to sustain her astern fortresses. The supply of recruits from home was uncertain. Yet permanent, continually replenished military forces had to be obtained. He therefore promoted the colonization of territory in the immediate hinterland of the forts, modest areas sufficient to provide local food supplies, and encouraged his men to marry girls of the various indigenous races, thereby enabling each settlement to have a permanent Christian population, raising sons for its own protection.

Malacca

The Portuguese endeavour now penetrated further east and nearer to the commercial crux of the matter—the Spice Islands. Between Goa and the islands of the Indies lay one last strategic port under Muslim control—Malacca, the most important port in South-East Asia. Like Socotra and Ormuz, it was situated at a controlling point on the main trade route. All commerce between the Spice Islands and Baghdad passed through the Strait of Malacca, which off the town itself is at its narrowest, a patrol ship mid-Strait being able to see Sumatra on one side and Lalaya on the other. Only by hugging the coast of Sumatra and making all sail could Arab and Indian traders hope to pass in safety a Malacca hostile to them.

In 1511, after a stiff fight, Albuquerque invested Malacca, which thenceforward became the advance eastern headquarters of Portuguese Asia, under a Captain-General responsible to the Viceroy at Goa. In Malacca the Portuguese once more installed themselves with forts, churches, and harbour works, creating in that beautiful place another Christian town, this time set in the changeless climate of the equator, with its warm, breezy days and cool nights.

Forcibly diverting spices and other merchandise from reaching the Middle East, by seizure and trickery the Portuguese obtained its flow along the sea route to Goa and Lisbon. Their conquest of Malacca also threw into their hands the considerable Eastward current of trade from Persia, Turkey, and the Arab cities, all of which they put to good account.

Jorge Alvares' voyage to China

On their earliest voyages to the Malabar coast of India, the Portuguese had heard of a mysterious, fair-skinned people called Chin, who many years ago, but just within living memory, had visited India and Ceylon in huge ships. Several times they had come, and then, no one knew why, their voyages had ceased.

While Albuquerque was in Malacca in 1511, it chanced that some large junks arrived in port. Albuquerque interviewed the masters and discovered that they were Chins. More than that— and one may well imagine the excitement of that far-distant shipboard evening—the Portuguese realized that the most celebrated of all European travellers' tales was not perhaps the myth so long supposed. In the person of these Chins they had reached out to the Cathay of Marco Polo. Typical of the age, this remarkable conclusion was conveyed to the King of Portugal and then kept secret, in suchwise that 200 years later, Europe was still arguing about whether, by some inconceivable chance, the China of porcelain, silk, and tea might be the same as Marco Polo's Cathay.

Finding the Chins to be forthright people, seemingly reliable in their dealings and, most important of all, not Muslims, Albuquerque decided that in addition to his main design of exploring the Indies, expeditions should be sent to Siam, whence some of the junks had come, and to the land of the Chins themselves, which here acquired its European name, China. The junkmasters agreed to carry a Portuguese mission to Siam, and with this encouragement one of Albuquerque's captains, Jorge Alvares, was in 1513 sent in a chartered Burmese vessel to find out what he could about, and if possible open trade with, the Chinese.

Alvares touched the coast of China at the country's great southern mouth, the Pearl River. In appearance it was much as it is today. Although fishermen and pirates had for centuries used its island anchorages, few of the islands themselves were inhabited. Such villages as existed, where the land was flat enough for a few fields of rice, were places of no consequence, grimly surrounded by granite hills. Neglected, remote, the outermost edge of Chinese civilization, the villages were some of them fortified, all with houses grouped close together facing the sea. Behind some were rugged groves of trees, maintained for good luck, and in sheltered valleys a few other hardy trees arose among rocks and small ravines. On hillsides catching the summer winds was nothing but coarse grass. In rain it would be hard to imagine a less inviting place. But under a blue sky, and despite the sea being brown with river silt, the gloomy islands became pale grass green tinged with subtle shades of purple, and the scene assumed an aspect of majesty and peace.

The newcomers anchored in what was then the most populous harbour, between the district town of Namtao and the island of Lintin, situated within the estuary. South of them, where the river meets the sea, rose the 3,000-foot peaks of Lantao Island, with somewhere among the islands east of it, not visible from the river, the island one day to be known as Hongkong. Far across on the west and less mountainous side of the estuary was a low, rocky peninsula, its only sign of habitation two small temples surrounded by trees. This was the future Macao.

Sixty-three miles from Namtao, up the estuary and river beyond, lay Canton, the largest city in South China, a cosmopolitan trading centre since very early times. Although Alvares was not allowed to go to Canton, he was well received by the Chinese, did a good trade, and returned reasonably satisfied to Malacca. He had discovered yet another unexpected and lucrative route with which Europe had no connexion.

Through Malacca there passed to Persia and Turkey regular cargoes of valuable Chinese goods, in particular porcelain and silk. In the opposite direction came Persian carpets, metalware and, from Indian ports, fine cotton, muslin and other luxury articles. To China came numbers of junks from Borneo and the Indies, bearing sandalwood and spices, for which in China there was even greater demand than there was in Europe. The bulk and real value of Asia's trade, as could now be appreciated, was between one Asian country and another, the merchandise going on the long journey to Venice being only a fraction of what the Portuguese found within their grasp. Not only were they able to inaugurate a new commerce between Europe and the East; in the East itself they replaced all others as the principal carriers from port to port.

Within a few years they were established in the Indies, with posts at Ternate in the Moluccas and Macassar in Celebes. Where they occupied no territory, they secured trading rights by treaty, thus extending their operations to Bengal, Burma, Siam, and Cochin-China.

All the costly goods Europe demanded from the East: pearls and brocades from China, superb batik and cloth of gold from Java, benzoin from Sumatra, rubies and scented woods from Burma, exquisitely woven scarves and vestments from Bengal, diamonds and sapphires from Ceylon, camphor from Borneo, nutmeg, cinnamon, and cloves from the Spice Islands, sandalwood from Timor, carpets from Persia, gold and silver from Ethiopia and India, and every imaginable kind of curiosity and ornament which the ingenuity of the East had devised: it all came in Portuguese ships to Lisbon, in quantities such as Europe had never known before, for sale at prices five times lower than in Venice. The medieval system of trade between West and East was broken, the Navigator's dream at Sagres unbelievably justified and fulfilled.

The first European envoy to Peking

The year after Jorge Alvares' voyage, a second venture was sent to China, this time under a kinsman of Christopher Columbus, the Italian captain Raffaelo Perestrello, who reached China in a chartered junk in 1514. These first two encounters with the Chinese having been encouraging, it was decided in Goa to follow the procedure adopted in the case of other non-Muslim countries by sending to the capital of China an envoy with instructions to conclude a trading agreement.

The envoy chosen was Tomé Pires, former apothecary to the Crown Prince of Portugal, and author of one of the great reference works of the period, the *Suma Oriental*, describing the eastern lands the Portuguese discovered, and who, in negotiating with any country other than the Celestial Empire, would surely have had every prospect of success. He embarked with his retinue as passengers in a Portuguese squadron sent in 1517 to trade in the Pearl River. The fleet, the first European ships to reach China, anchored off Namtao before being allowed to sail up-river to Canton, where the envoy was put ashore, a house being provided for him by the Chinese authorities. The following year, with the steady winter wind blowing southward, the fleet sailed back to Malacca, leaving Pires still negotiating to reach the capital.

China was used to receiving foreign missions. Tibet, Burma, Siam, the Indo-Chinese countries, and Central Asian states all sent them from time to time. They were described as missions of tribute-bearing barbarians, the Chinese theory being that China was the only civilized state on earth, of which it was the centre. Magnanimous rules existed for the proper conduct of missions. Canton being one of the principal cities through which embassies entered China and waited for permission to proceed to Peking, Pires' arrival was in conformity with precedent, the only difficulty being that the Chinese officials concerned had never heard of Goa or Portugal. They had to be happy in their minds that such places did in fact exist, because the Imperial Court would have similar doubts, and mistakes on such matters were not tolerated. After waiting in Canton for *two years* while this and various other matters were discussed, Pires was finally allowed to travel northward by the long and slow canal route inland, again, the official route for embassies.

The Emperor Chang Tê (1506–21) was visiting Nanking, the Southern Capital, about halfway between Canton and Peking, his visit coinciding with the mission's arrival. When the Emperor was on tour, the extreme formality of the Court was relaxed. Chang Tê, a genial, easy-going person, received the Portuguese, treated them with every kindness, played games at a table with Pires, asked questions about his country, inspected the envoy's presents, and all his clothes and personal possessions as well, and arranged that the mission should go on to Peking, where later in the year he would see them again. In high hopes they proceeded to Peking and waited; but when early next year the Emperor returned, he did so only to die unexpectedly within a couple of days.

With their patron out of the way, the Portuguese became the victims of a Court intrigue that had been going on for years, the antagonists being the palace eunuchs and high members of

11

the civil service (the mandarins). In the last century, during the reign of Yung Lo (1403–24), the Court eunuchs, cultivating an interest in foreign countries, had organized the immense naval expeditions that had made the Chinese known as far abroad as Ceylon, the Malabar coast, and Arabia. Later, the strait-laced, traditionalist civil service promoted a successful reaction in favour of seclusion. Chang Tê's interest in Pires aroused civil service disapproval—it smacked of the Yung Lo epoch—and on the question of an audience with the new emperor, Ch'ia Ching, their opportunity came of asserting the dignity of the celestial Empire, as opposed to the frivolous informality tolerated by the eunuchs.

The mission's documents were re-examined. Surprise was expressed that the letter to the Emperor was written only by a subordinate (the Viceroy at Goa) and in language inadmissible in a communication addressed to the Son of Heaven. When barbarian kings addressed the Son of Heaven they did so personally, in terms of the deepest humility, not in this (as a European diplomatic document seemed to them) egalitarian tone. The suggestion was that Pires was an impostor, posing cleverly as a tribal envoy in order to gain admittance to the Heavenly Presence.

Since to admit to the Court that they had allowed an impostor to reach Peking would involve them in trouble, the officials had to proceed cautiously. With the excuse that it was not correct procedure for embassies to await the Emperor's pleasure in Peking itself, the Westerners were sent back to Canton until it be made known whether Ch'ia Ching would receive them.

In Canton, Portuguese prospects had deteriorated. A year earlier, while a number of their vessels were anchored off Namtao, a Chinese official had been assaulted by one Simão Peres de Andrade. The ships had been allowed to sail away unmolested, but the affair, duly reported to Peking, caused a bad impression. Eight months later, Portuguese merchants trading at Namtao, when informed that as a consequence of the Emperor's death all foreign shipping must leave China, had refused to depart until their cargoes, already promised, were put aboard. Several Portuguese were in consequence taken prisoner, some vessels being fired on as they approached to aid their countrymen.

It was to this deteriorated situation that Tomé Pires returned in Canton, where he and his staff were kept confined to their house, waiting through the winter for permission to go up again to Peking. Meanwhile from Goa a large squadron set sail under the command of Martim Afonso de Melo Coutinho, who also had instructions to make a treaty of peace and trade with China. In Malacca the Captain-General urgently advised them to proceed no further, lest they damage the prospects of Pires' mission, but Melo Coutinho, intent on the commercial profits of a voyage to China, took no notice. On arrival in the Pearl River in 1522, his ships were attacked by a fleet of Chinese war junks, and an attempt to land at Namtao met with popular hostility, obliging the Portuguese to withdraw. The squadron finally fought its way out to sea with the loss of two ships.

This incident sealed the fate of the Portuguese diplomatic mission. The Portuguese, in the Chinese assessment, were a dangerous tribe whose activities, evidently piratical, were not to be encouraged. Tomé Pires and his entourage were thrown into prison. Some were later executed; the rest are thought to have died in captivity. It was hardly an auspicious beginning to European diplomatic relations with China.

Effect of success on Portugal—Magellan's desertion to Spain
Meanwhile, great changes had taken place in Portugal since the wealth of the Indies first began to reach Lisbon. The country

was rapidly demoralized by its fabulous success. Agriculture and other normal forms of husbandry were neglected. With money pouring into Lisbon from all over Western Europe in exchange for spices and oriental goods, it was easier to purchase domestic requirements from abroad, rather than produce them by wearisome labour at home. With spend-thrift carelessness, Portugal began selling her splendid eastern wares to Antwerp in exchange for meat, corn, cheese, butter, and even chickens and eggs. Young men deserted their fields and villages in their thousands to take part in the eastern voyages, on which great numbers died. Imported Muslim and negro slaves from Africa, an important outcome of the voyages, to some extent replaced them at home; but thereby even more manual and menial work was taken out of Portuguese hands, increasing indolence and neglect of the land.

The plentiful supply of spices from the East caused prices in Europe to fall, and profits from voyages declined sharply. The sale of the cargo of pepper, cloves, and cinnamon which Vasco da Gama brought back from his first journey to India raised a sum sixty times greater than the entire cost of the voyage; but even before the end of the reign of Manuel I (1495–1521) such profits were a thing of the past. Pepper fell from 80 cruzados per quintal to 20 cruzados. Venice was reduced to a minor port, but Portugal did not benefit by her decline.

There can be few cases in history where the acquisition of wealth sowed such quickly-sprouting seeds of decline as happened in Portugal within ten years of the foundation of Goa. Commercially inexperienced, carried away by vainglorious confidence, and with a failure to grasp economic actualities, the Portuguese held that the fall in profits could only be offset by increasing the number of expeditions sent to the East. To finance these from a dwindling treasury, the King raised loans from Antwerp bankers and merchants. When, as was inevitable, profits dropped still more, Portugal fell more and more into debt.

The capital outlay required to finance sufficient voyages to meet the people's demand for them soon exceeded the royal capacity. In the hope of balancing the decline in profits by a greater trade and more discoveries, King Manuel withdrew his monopoly control, permitting private traders to finance their own expeditions. The resulting decrease in naval supervision of the trade route down the West African coast opened the way for numerous pirates, prominent among whom were the French. The dangers of the journey east increased; total losses became more frequent. By the early years of the reign of João III (1521–57) it was realized that Portugal had taken on more than she could carry. Several fortified posts on the west coast of Africa were abandoned, the forces manning them being diverted to Brazil, which seemed to be a more profitable region of enterprise than the East, and certainly a less distant one.

At the same time, far away in the Spice Islands, the contacts established by Portugal were threatened by Spain. With a view to limiting a dangerous rivalry between the two countries, the Borgia Pope Alexander VI had in 1494 divided between them, along a line which came to pass longitudinally 370 leagues west of the Azores, authority over all new-discovered lands. To the East of this line—this included Brazil, the discovery of which the Portuguese evidently kept secret until then—was Portugal's sphere, to the west Spain's.

That a pope, by drawing a line down the Atlantic Ocean, should divide the world between two nations has often been ridiculed since. At the time it was a very sensible arrangement. Confirmed by the two countries in the Treaty of Tordesillas, it might have been satisfactory as a means of keeping the peace, had it not been for the dissatisfaction of one outstanding Portuguese captain, Fernão de Magalhães, known in English as Magellan. Having served under Albuquerque at the taking of Malacca, Magellan returned to Portugal, where on account of certain misdemeanours committed by him in India, his application for a pension as a nobleman attendant at Court was refused. Disgruntled, he transferred his services to the Emperor Charles V, took Spanish nationality in 1517, and with the knowledge he had already gained of the East, set out to reach the Spice Islands by a westerly route across the South Atlantic and Pacific Oceans, the direction technically allowed for Spanish ships. In 1521, having rounded the foot of South America through the straits that today bear his name, Magellan reached the islands later to be named the Philippines. In an attempt to bring them under Spanish suzerainty he was opposed and killed by the forces of the Raja of Mactan, a small island near Cebu; but his comrades, continuing the voyage, finally reached the much-desired Moluccas.

During the next thirty-five years, other Spanish expeditions were sent with varying fortunes to resume contact with the Philippines, and in the Moluccas there were frequent fights between Spaniards and Portuguese. Not only therefore was Portugal at home lightly throwing away the fruits of her immense enterprise; in the East her position, even before it was fully established, was being assailed by another European state.

2

Squatters on the China Coast

With overseas Chinese in illicit trade—Liampo

After the failure of Tomé Pires' mission to China, no further official attempts were made to open trade with that country. But with the withdrawal of the royal monopoly of trade to the East, privateers operating from Malacca became free to try their luck in China, which quite a few of them, dissatisfied with the various restrictive conditions their government still placed on trade through Malacca, now proceeded to do. This brought them in touch with the overseas Chinese communities in South-East Asia, most of whom were engaged in the same trade, all of it forbidden by the laws of China, which allowed no foreign trade except with tribute-paying barbarians such as the Siamese.

To understand this extraordinary position, that even overseas Chinese were not permitted to trade with their mother country, we must look back for a moment into the past. Chinese trade with neighbouring countries—Luzon, Borneo, Timor, Indo-China, and the Indies—is very old, and had resulted in a small flow of Chinese emigration from the provinces of Fukien and Kwangtung, a movement which, much later on, received a great stimulus from the voyages of the Yung Lo period. In 1431, a few years after Yung Lo's death, this expansive period of China's foreign policy came abruptly to an end. No more overseas expeditions were financed, Chinese ships were no longer allowed to sail abroad, and the death penalty was imposed on any Chinese attempting to leave the country.

The great expense of the organized expeditions was obviously a prime reason for this. Another appears to have been, as mentioned earlier, that in the intrigues of the Court the civil servants got the better of the eunuchs, and restored a more traditional policy. But the most significant cause was undoubtedly the governmental alarm aroused by the increased scale of emigration, which it was thought would result in an outward flow of silver, to the country's detriment.

Whatever stabilizing effects the edict may have had on China's internal economy, its international outcome could not have been more decisive. The Eastern seas, which for thirty years had been pacified by the fear inspired by China's tremendous demonstrations of naval might, were suddenly left free for all. Within a year or so, Japanese and Formosan smugglers and pirates were active—as they had been before— along the China coast; and they were not the only ones. Many of them were dependent for their livelihood on trade with China. There was little point in their going back to China if they were never to be allowed to leave again. The great majority, therefore, remained in the lands of their adoption. While the situation invited illegal trade, China's poor coastal defences invited smugglers and pirates. Pirate ships, in fact, frequently operated as carriers, being particularly sought after by merchants because of their effective armament.

It was into this dangerous and uncertain trade that the Portuguese entered after the failure of the Pires mission. If the Chinese would not legalize foreign commerce, the alternative for Portuguese privateers lay in illegal trade, with the possibility that such contacts might lead in the course of time to an opportunity of establishing themselves on a legal footing.

Avoiding the Pearl River because of their earlier troubles there, they made their way up the coast as far as the mouth of the Yangtse, often with Chinese guides and passengers aboard. One or two places in Kwangtung and Fukien were found to be possible for trade, and in 1540, again with the assistance of Chinese merchants engaged in the illicit foreign trade, they began wintering regularly on an island off the Chekiang coast—opposite the Chusan group of islands—not far from the mouth of the Yung river.

This place was known as Liampo, and was the first European settlement in China, if settlement is not perhaps too grand a word for it.

On early European maps of China one finds Liampo marked in huge letters, as if it were one of the largest cities in the East. Actually it was a collection of matshed huts, a precarious residence of smugglers living ashore. The large letters honourably accorded to it on old maps signify its importance relative strictly to Europeans. At last they had obtained a slender footing in China.

Japan—destruction of Liampo—Sanchuang

This was only the beginning of their luck. Two years after the 'foundation' of Liampo—bringing us to 1542—Fernão Mendes Pinto, famous to later generations as the author of one of the most exciting travel books ever written, *A Peregrinação*, making his way to Liampo with a fellow-adventurer in a Chinese junk, was driven far off course by a storm, eventually landing on the island of Tanegashima, south of Kyushu. By accident they had discovered Japan.

Here, quite unlike the experience of their comrades in China, they were hospitably received by local rulers and their subjects, excited great curiosity, and with their arquebuses, the first firearms ever seen in Japan, created a sensation which spread throughout the country.

They discovered that in Japan there was tremendous demand for Chinese goods. China's refusal to allow trade with the Japanese, whom the Chinese particularly detested, had created extraordinary profits in the illicit trade between the two countries. As Mendes Pinto and his friend saw at once, if

19

Portuguese ships could break into this, there were easy fortunes to be made. Greatly excited, the two adventurers resumed their voyage to Liampo.

Within a few months, news of their discovery, and of the immense possibilities it opened was brought to Malacca and Goa. A Portuguese ship was at once sent to Japan, this voyage being the beginning of seasonal trade between Malacca, Liampo, and various Japanese ports on the island of Kyushu. The Japanese paid for their imports in silver, with which the Portuguese, to their great advantage, purchased from the Chinese at Liampo the silk and porcelain they needed for export both westward and eastward, to Malacca and to Japan.

This new line of trade was getting under way in flourishing style, when in 1547 a new Governor of Fukien and Chekiang was appointed, determined to stamp out illicit trade. The Governor, Chü Yuan, made careful preparations, and in 1549, when Portuguese ships called at Liampo, the shore settlement and ships were set upon unexpectedly, the settlement was destroyed, several Portuguese were captured, and many of their Chinese associates either killed or imprisoned.

This setback, greatly magnified in transmission, caused consternation in Malacca, and in some old accounts reads almost like a national disaster. But whereas after the failure of the Pires mission, Malacca and Goa had been disinclined to pursue contacts with so unpredictable and difficult a country as China, reaction to this second setback was different. The newly found Japan trade was a silver mine far too lucrative to be abandoned. It was decided that the Chekiang coast would have to be avoided in future, while trade with Japan must somehow be maintained. Since a sheltering and revictualling place was necessary somewhere on the long route between Malacca and Japan, and Chinese silk was essential to the Japan trade, this meant that contact with China could not be abandoned. Accordingly, avoiding Chekiang, attention was once again shifted southwards to where the Portuguese first started, in Kwangtung.

Rather than risk the uncertainties of a site near the Pearl River, the traders chose a small island called Sanchuang, fifty-two miles southwest of the river. They named it euphonically São Joã, or St John Island. Here to their surprise they succeeded in coming to 'some sort of understanding . . . with the Chinese officials', the island quickly replacing Liampo as the port of call for trade with Japan, and in a distinctly better atmosphere of understanding.

It was not until long after that the reason for this improved attitude became known. Some years earlier, in 1530, the Canton merchants had petitioned the Governor of Kwangtung and Kwangsi for the re-opening of their city to foreign traders. It chanced that Lin Fu, the Governor, was concurrently President of the Board of Censors, a position of the greatest influence, the Censors being privileged to receive, examine, and present to the Emperor all criticisms and complaints, however unsavoury. Lin memorialized the Throne, complaining of the shortage of tropical spices and the loss of revenue from customs dues; and in spite of strong Court opposition to foreign trade, the tone of the reply he received was conciliatory. The principle of commerce with foreign countries was accepted. Europeans and Japanese (feringhis and 'dwarf robbers') were still specifically debarred from trading, leaving by implication only the minor commerce of the Siamese, and in a sense the overseas Chinese. But it was a symptom of change.

Nineteen years later, after the destruction of Liampo, influential Fukien merchants, faced with ruin by the cessation of their overseas commerce, made similar demands, and in a memorial to the Throne complained of Chü Yuan's action. The Emperor Ch'ia Ching (1521–67) instituted an inquiry, as a result

21

of which, for unjustifiably executing Chinese merchants, the Governor was condemned to be conveyed to Peking in chains, several other officials were either banished or dismissed from the civil service, and the release of Chinese and Portuguese prisoners was authorized. Chü Yuan, rather than disgrace his family's name, committed suicide.

Report of these orders and events quickly reached Kwangtung, producing an understandable reaction among Chinese officials. The Portuguese presence on Sanchuang was tolerated.

St Francis Xavier

Sanchuang was not used for more than three seasons. Its claim to remembrance rests not on any merits it may have possessed as a settlement—for it is a grassy, windswept place affording little shelter to ships or men,—but on its connexion with one of the great men of the age, the so-called Apostle of the East, St Francis Xavier.

In that Macao was to be as much a religious centre as a commercial one, this will be an appropriate moment to take a look at the part missionaries were playing in these early days of the European connexion with the Far East.

Of the numerous popular misconceptions concerning the Portuguese empire, none crops up more frequently than the assertion that the Portuguese advanced designedly upon the East as colonizers, with sword in one hand and Bible in the other. Even from the few pages preceding this, it can be observed that there was very little design about it. The Portuguese possessions came into being as a result of fortuities and necessities of the moment; and it is important to remember that wherever Asian princes were friendly and disposed to trade with them, the Portuguese established only such lightly protected places as were required to secure their goods from petty marauders.

The superbly-built Portuguese fortresses, which are still to be seen right across Asia, at first give the impression of a sternly military organization, trading with the East and imposing its will by force. This was not quite how it was at the time. With the seas infested with pirates, and with the Portuguese, as strangers, naturally subject to the intrigues of Asian kings and their courts, strong protection was essential. But it was only required in emergencies. With their characteristically easy-going temperament, the concept of a trading empire imposed by military force was alien to the Portuguese.

Nor had they any intention of conquering large tracts of territory. The boundaries of the present state of Malacca, extending nowhere more than twenty miles inland from the port, typify their territorial aims, which were simply to have Portuguese-protected areas to provide their ports with a sure supply of meat, milk, and vegetables, together with a source of local manpower. Though proudly named '*conquistas*', the territories were modest affairs. Trade was the thing; the port and its requirements came first.

Systematic conquest, with the joint aims of colonizing foreign lands and converting their native populations to Christianity, was a Spanish concept, first put into practice in Asia a little later, when in 1565 Luzon and its hundreds of smaller companion islands, the Philippines, were brought under the dominion of Spain.

Nevertheless, the age in which the Portuguese entered the Far East was the age in which the vision of a universal Christian state appeared to intellectual Europe as a realizable goal. With the Portuguese traders came the missionaries, and where the traders established themselves ashore, the missionaries did likewise. But it was not a jointly planned assault on the East. The captains and the missionaries each had their own separate interests, and these not infrequently conflicted. The captains of those times welcomed priests in their ships; they were required by the King to carry them. But a priest aboard a Portuguese ship was seldom permitted to celebrate Mass at sea; it was considered unlucky. Once arrived safely at a destination, such community of interest as existed was often dissipated, as is exemplified in the tribulations of St Francis Xavier in the last years of his life.

Impelled by the aim of the universal Christian state, Francis Xavier, one of the first members of the Society of Jesus, had spent the years 1549–51 in Japan, in an attempt to convert that country to Christianity. There he had reached the conclusion that the key to the conversion of the Far East lay in China, to which Japan and other countries looked with such deep respect and admiration that, only if China set the lead, the rest of the Far East might be persuaded to follow. Returning to Goa in 1551, the Saint persuaded the Viceroy to send another mission to China, the first since that of Tomé Pires, this time with the joint aims of concluding a treaty of trade and friendship, and allowing the Christian faith to be preached.

While in Japan, Francis Xavier had occasioned the Portuguese traders some embarrassment by his outspoken condemnation of Japanese immorality, and among a number of traders he was, though respected as a priest, to some extent *mal vu*, as being a source of political trouble damaging to commerce. When therefore the China mission, bearing Francis Xavier with it, reached Malacca, the Captain-General, with this and also the known dangers of negotiating with China in mind, refused to allow the mission to proceed. The Saint, who did not take kindly to opposition, went on with a few companions aboard a trading ship to Sanchuang, where he tried to enlist the support of the traders in obtaining permission to enter China.

Here again he encountered trouble of the same kind. The consequences of this dynamic and intolerant missionary having dealings with Chinese officials at this delicate juncture, when things were at last showing signs of improvement, were considered too dangerous for the more experienced merchants to contemplate. Little help was given therefore, and in December 1552 Francis Xavier died in a hut on the island—not exactly a story of sword in one hand and Bible in the other.

The Apostle of the East, who for all the reservations some might have had about him, was nonetheless recognized by his contemporaries as one of the outstanding figures of the age, was first buried on Sanchuang, to which pilgrimages from Macao and later from Hongkong were made, until under the communist government of China such expeditions were no longer possible. Later his body was transferred to Malacca, where in the nave of the ruined church of St Paul the place of its temporary interment can still be seen. Miraculously preserved, the body finally reached its present resting-place at Goa.

Beginning of legal trade at Canton—pirates

During the three years following the Saint's death, Leonel de Sousa, one of the principal captains, by steady perseverance and something approaching the proper Chinese use of go-betweens and gifts, succeeded in coming to a verbal agreement with the Marine Superintendent at Canton, whereby Portuguese ships might trade openly in the ports of Kwangtung, on condition they paid the normal taxes and came and went in peace.

To say they bribed their way in would not be correct, in that the gifts they made were not considered in China as bribes. Purchase their way in, however, they certainly did. There was no other way. And the gifts coming from the Chinese merchant go-betweens, the situation conformed with usage.

Thus, in 1555, they went up to Canton for the first of what thenceforth were seasonal visits. Missionaries were also admitted. One of the joyful moments of the first trip was the rediscovery of the prisoners from Liampo, who under the Emperor's orders had been released with the Chinese arrested, and had since made their way as best they could in China.

The traders' position was now very favourable, and a fortuity was to render it even more so. The years 1553–6 witnessed at least two formidable descents of pirates from the Ryukyu Islands. Actually they were not pirates in the strict sense of the word. They were armed robbers. They arrived in fleets and terrorized the coast, plundering, looting, and destroying. Numerous villages along this particular part of the coast, including some on Kowloon peninsula, lost everything they possessed.

At some stage—it is not known exactly when or where—these marauders encountered Portuguese armed vessels which gave them the punishment of their lives. This is evident not from documents, but from study of the surrounding circumstances, and it greatly enhanced the Portuguese position in respect of Chinese officialdom.

Lampakkau—foundation of Macao

In 1553 Sanchuang was abandoned, its anchorage being too exposed, and the traders moved slightly nearer the Pearl River, to an island with a shallow, protected anchorage in the delta of the West River, which comes down by many courses due south of Canton, through riverine districts bordering the west bank of the greater Pearl River. This next settlement was known as Lampakkau (in Chinese the characters make the sense Wave-white Inlet or Creek), and although it was never more than a matshed establishment it was a large one, numbering over 400 huts. As in many instances before and since, whatever the attitude of their officials might be, ordinary Chinese merchants, boat-owners, fishermen, and menials were attracted to the

Westerners and the wealth their presence brought. Within a few weeks of moving, the Portuguese found as their neighbours a swiftly enlarging Chinese wood and matshed village.

Lampakkau is no longer distinguishable as an island, the waters round it having silted up. Nineteen miles to the north-east of it, on the last strip of solid ground separating the deltaic region from the broad estuary of the Pearl River, was another convenient anchorage. It had a choice of two natural harbours, one—an inner harbour—on the West River, the other—an outer harbour—in a fine bay facing the Pearl River. South of it were some sheltering islands. The Portuguese had already visited the place in 1534 and 1535, and during the year 1555, when Lampakkau was their principal base, this still more convenient anchorage was used with greater frequency. Characteristically, that celebrated 'first' in so many Portuguese doings, Fernão Mendes Pinto, is the first known person to have written a letter from this new anchorage, the letter being dated 1555 and headed with the name that now enters history—Macao. In the winter of 1556–7 actual settlement began on the narrow peninsula between the two harbours, and Portuguese Macao came into being.

Tradition asserts that the traders received Chinese permission to settle at Macao as a reward for their action in the suppression of pirates. This tradition seems to contain the truth. The Ryukyu pirates have already been mentioned. In addition, there was evidently a major encounter around 1556–7 with a Chinese horde commanded by a notorious pirate chief, who was completely worsted. 'For this reason,' an early Jesuit account states, 'the Portuguese were brought nearer to Canton, as the elders of the city testify.' What apparently happened was that the Chinese—and by this is meant the minor officials with whom the traders had dealings in the coastal region—were so impressed by Portuguese efficiency in dealing with pirates that they suggested the traders give up Lampakkau entirely, and concentrate on Macao, strategically placed as it is to prevent access to Canton. The Pearl River at its mouth is twenty miles wide, and with the great city of Canton as its prize it was one of the most dangerously vulnerable places on the South China coast. It was of course a major target for pirates, and had been for centuries. Not for nothing are the islands off the river mouth called the Ladrones (*ladrões*, robbers).

The traders were already using Macao informally as an alternative to Lampakkau, and in 1557, by what was clearly the general wish of local officials and of the people who actually lived there, the peninsula became their headquarters. Shortly after this, permission of a more formal nature was received from Canton for them to stay there, though exactly in what form and from whom is not known, and work immediately began on the erection of permanent buildings.

Curiously enough, there is no known Chinese official reference to Portuguese help in curbing piracy during this particular period 1556–7, though there is abundant written evidence, in particular from Chinese clan records, that this was a time of frightful danger along the ill-protected coast. The well-armed Portuguese were a welcome safeguard. Fernão Mendes Pinto, who was there at the time, refers to 'the year 1557 [when] the mandarins of Canton, at the request of the local inhabitants, gave us this port of Macao.' This implies very general agreement. The Portuguese had won their way in by establishing themselves as friends.

Considering that China was the most difficult of all countries to have dealings with, Portuguese establishment in Macao, in tacit concord and understanding, ranks as one of the most remarkable moments in the annals of East and West.

The earliest firm evidence of Portuguese assistance against pirates occurs a few years later, in 1564. On this occasion, several hundred Chinese soldiers on garrison duties on various coastal islands deserted, having received no pay, and turning pirate, proceeded to maraud petty traders going by boat to Canton. With nine ships, they finally threatened the city itself, preventing all access to it by water. An attack was prepared against them, the official in charge being one Yu Tai-yau, who reported that 'foreigners have offered to help, and if the foreigners should prove successful, the foreign leader will be handsomely rewarded, although there is no Imperial decree authorizing them to pay tribute.'

The Portuguese did help. Loading their cannon in Chinese junks as a ruse, they approached the pirates who, expecting Chinese methods of encounter, attempted to close with them. Only too late, at close quarters, the Western cannons were sighted. At their first burst of fire there was panic in the pirate ships, men hurling themselves into the sea to escape. The result was a total rout, with no losses on the Portuguese side.

With deeds such as this to their credit, the Portuguese achieved what amounted to local indispensability. They were the most experienced mariners in the world, used to dealing with pirates the best part of the way from Morocco to Japan. Chinese government forces being totally inadequate, permission was given to the Portuguese to settle at the river mouth. As they were not—as the Siamese were, for instance—tribute-paying foreigners, their position from the viewpoint of the Chinese civil service was irregular, and no formal agreement could be made with them. But agreement of some kind there must have been, otherwise it is impossible to explain why, from the outset, permanent buildings were erected at Macao, when none had ever been erected at the earlier settlements, Liampo, Sanchuang, and Lampakkau.

Concerning the agreement's form and contents, Chinese official records have so far revealed nothing. From Portuguese records it appears that a document of some kind—an illuminated scroll, or possibly a banner of silk with writing on it—was presented to the Portuguese community in appreciation of their defeat of the pirates. Another document gave them permission to reside at Macao, the characters of this communication being carved in stone and wood in the Senate House. The scroll was lost, the old Senate House burnt, and no record of the exact Chinese wording survives. Few Portuguese, then or now, could read Chinese, and it is probable that even when the carved characters were in existence, few understood exactly what they meant.

The Chinese accepted the situation as an expedience at once practical and astute, setting barbarians at the very mouth of the great river to defend it from other barbarians, namely 'dwarf robbers' (Japanese) and pirates in general. At first, too, probably no one envisaged Macao being more than a matshed settlement, like Liampo and Lampakkau. By the time it was realized in Peking that a rich city had grown up, the profits China was drawing from it, in taxation and trade, were so advantageous that it would have been pointless—as well as difficult—to have interfered.

The Chinese conceded nothing of importance. In their view, the peninsula was a fractional part of their country in which non-tribute-paying foreigners, on payment of the normal taxes, were allowed to settle. The Portuguese however, though they paid the taxes, claimed that a concession had been made, giving them sovereign rights over the place. Upon this divergence of view the city of Macao arose.

3
The Golden Age of the Japan Trade

Macao's peculiar independence

The acquisitions of Macao meant more to the Portuguese than gaining a rocky ledge on which to build themselves homes, warehouses, and churches. Without any of the bargaining or discussion that usually precedes the award of such privileges, they had acquired the monopoly of the entire maritime trade of China. Chinese were forbidden to leave the coast; Japanese were forbidden to enter Chinese ports; Arabs, who had once had a resident population in Canton, had been ejected from the trade routes in the course of Portugal's curbing of Islam; Siamese and other nearby peoples could still come to China if they wished, but their vessels were so small that they were no longer of any significance in international trade. The Portuguese had become the carriers for all large-scale commerce in the Far East, and in the fabulous trade with Japan they were in unassailed monopoly control.

The caravel, principal vessel of the early Discoveries, had by this time been replaced by the *nao*, later versions of which were called in English the carrack, which for size, strength, capacity, and armament was the foremost ship on the seas. A carrack could measure anything up to 900 tons, and was easily identifiable by its high forecastle and stern, having in the distance a curvature like a floating crescent, a form which impressed oriental artists, and made its way into the contemporary art of Bengal and Japan.

The discovery of the quality of teak for use in shipbuilding led to the foundation of important shipyards on the west coast of India, at Goa, Cochin, and Bassein. From these yards the finest carracks of all were made, at moderate prices.

In spite of deteriorated conditions in Portugal, the future of Portuguese Asia seemed momentarily secure. The only foreseeable rival, Spain, had suffered repeated losses in attempting trade and colonization in the Spice Islands and the Philippines, the most recent Spanish expedition, under Ruy Lopez de Villalobos, having surrendered to the Portuguese in the Moluccas, Villalobos himself dying at Amboina in 1546.

But in including Macao with Portuguese Asia there is an important reservation to be made. The Portuguese traders to China and Japan, the men who had edged into the illegal trade and gradually created for their activities a status of legitimacy, formed amongst their fellow-countrymen in the East a separate cadre. The long and determined effort to break down the opposition of the Chinese government, the tenacious squatting at various places on the China coast, the discovery of Japan: this was the work of individual traders acting on their own initiative, with the knowledge of, but without specific orders from, the Viceroy at Goa or the Captain-General at Malacca; and although the government sent Leonel de Sousa to negotiate with the Chinese, the outcome of his negotiations was interpreted by the China coast individualists as their own triumph, not Goa's.

When a year after the start of legitimate trade, they gained permission to build a proper settlement at Macao, it was again a feat of the men on the spot. Goa did not authorize the foundation of Macao. Goa was informed, some months after the event, that Macao had been founded.

No officers being at Macao with proper instructions, the administration of the place began under a committee of the principal traders; and by the time officials were appointed by Goa this committee, called the Senate, was an established institution, which the Macanese had no intention of giving up. Macao thus did not quite fit into the bureaucratic pattern of

Portuguese Asia. Its citizens sedulously protected their measure of independence, and in the centuries ahead, conflicts between the city elders and the officials appointed by Goa to be in charge of administration were frequent.

A certain degree of control was of course maintained, even from the earliest days of the city. This was due to the Captain-Major of the annual voyage to Japan being an official appointee. Since the Portuguese possessions depended on trade to finance administration, defence, shipbuilding and other requirements, it was considered important to limit independent trade as far as possible. Certain valuable commodities were a royal monopoly, and at all times the right to trade in the East was reserved to the government, to apportion as it saw fit.

For traders owning their own vessels this was no great deprivation—except in the case of the most daring individualists—since it was an obvious safeguard to travel with the well-armed government fleet. The Captain-Major was empowered to permit approved private traders to join the voyage. For each permission given, he received either an outright gift or a percentage of the profits, which went into his own purse. The post of Captain-Major, from this and from the private trade he could do on his own account, was a lucrative one, generally reserved for friends or relatives of the Viceroy.

This was really the only hold the bureaucracy of Goa and Malacca had over their foster-child on the China coast. Macao, a sturdy orphan and a very rich one, was an anomaly from the start, a colony without a governor.

Camões

Fernão Mendes Pinto is not the only famous name in Portuguese literature to be associated with Macao in its earliest days. Beside his stands the greatest name of all, Luis Vaz de Camões. Local tradition holds strongly that Camões was in Macao in the year

33

of its foundation, engaged while there on writing his masterpiece, *Os Lusiadas*. It is thought that for a few months in Macao during 1557 Camões held the post of Trustee for the Dead and Absent, an appointment needed by every settlement in those dangerous times.

Camões, who in character was a Portuguese mixture of Benvenuto Cellini and Sir Richard Burton, was as incisive with his sword as he was with his pen. Mainly for his political lampoons, read out at street-corners in the days before newspapers, he was ordered out of Lisbon, taking part in one of Portugal's North African campaigns, where he lost an eye. Later, arrested for duelling—a lady was involved—in the streets of Lisbon, he was 'banished' to Goa, where his jibes so infuriated the local authorities that he was told he would be spared imprisonment only if he exiled himself to the furthest ends of the Portuguese empire, China and Japan.

This sentence, instead of breaking his spirit, rendered him immortal. His immense journeys awakened him to the true greatness of his country's achievement, and gave birth to his *Os Lusiadas*, an epic poem recounting Vasco da Gama's voyage to India, written in a strange mixture of the chevaleresque, the baroque, and the exotic finely observed, in which while medieval paladins are guided across the oceans by gods and zephyrs of pagan mythology, many of the cantos tingle with the authentic tropical atmosphere of swooning palm trees, the lustre of oriental Courts, and the scent of ships and spices. On one occasion, shipwrecked off the mouth of the Mekong river in Indo-China, the poet, up to his neck in water, managed to wade ashore holding aloft his precious manuscript.

The poem was published in Lisbon in 1572, and was at once recognized as the paean—perhaps also the last post—of the great age which by then had already passed away. But while it won Camões respect, it earned him little or no money. He died in Lisbon in complete poverty six years later, deserted by all he knew save a negress from a nearby street who attended his last hours. Almost prophetically, the year of his death, 1578, saw the most frightful disaster in Portuguese history.

In Macao his name is associated with a group of monolithic boulders on a slight wooded hill at the north end of the inner harbour wharves. What exactly the association was no one knows. Some say he wrote there. More likely it was his preferred evening stroll, a good vantage point to enjoy the view and the summer breeze. Those who decry the tradition of his stay sometimes point in substantiation to the fact that Camões never referred to Macao in his writings. But this is not surprising. All he would have seen of the place in 1557 would have been an uninspiring expanse of matsheds, bamboo scaffolding and rapidly rising stone walls, with no certainty of continued development, and at that time no officially confirmed status— confirmed in Goa, that is to say—of Macao as a Portuguese possession.

A 1613 Lisbon edition of *Os Lusiadas* states in a foreword that the poet visited the Far East, which in the geography of the day means that he visited Macao. If, as Macao tradition holds, this visit took place in 1557—and this seems not likely when taken in connexion with the few known facts of Camões' life,— he would have been engaged on his great poem at this time, and it would have been when leaving Macao that the shipwreck incident took place, recorded in the magnificent tenth canto of the epic. The tradition of his stay in Macao is very old. The first written reference to the bouldered hill occurs in an undated entry, *circa* 1631–5, in the register of the Jesuit seminary. This records the sale of 'some land known as the Rocks of Camões', adding the location, which accords with the rocks that bear his name today.

The city's rapid growth

Apart from the two Chinese temples referred to earlier, Macao when the Portuguese moved in was largely uninhabited, an irregular chain of low but surprisingly steep hills and boulders, with coarse shrubs and stunted trees growing wherever there was protection from the winds.

Both temples survive to this day. The northern one, Buddhist in character and dedicated to Kwan Yin, the Goddess of Mercy, was situated beyond the zone of original Portuguese settlement, at a location called Mong Ha, where there was a Chinese village. It was in one of the courtyards of this temple that the first treaty between China and the United States of America was signed.

The southern temple, close to the foot of the Peninsula, shielded by a grove of dark-leafed Chinese banyans and by imposing boulders on a steeply rising hill, is the fishermen's temple which gave its name to the city.

The fishermen whom the Portuguese came across there were originally coastal migrants from Fukien. Some centuries earlier, the first of them had been caught in a typhoon and driven far from their familiar fishing grounds. Being in dire peril, they offered prayers to Ma Cho, the Ancestral Grandmother, patroness of seafarers, and reached land at this sheltered spot where they and their ships were safe. In gratitude they made a shrine to Ma Cho, whom they held in the greatest veneration, believing she had personally saved them. The shrine was in due course enlarged into a temple, which was the community's focal point ashore.

Their name for the place in Fukienese was Ma Cho Kau, the Inlet or Creek of the Ancestral Grandmother, and an abbreviated form of this—Ma Kau—became the name of the city. The inescapable Chinese affix 'Ah' somehow got attached to it, and the earliest Portuguese name for the place was Amacao.

Chinese place-names, later to become street-names, in this particular area indicate that by 1557, and probably long before that date, the Fukienese community were living partly afloat, as most fishermen in South China do, and partly ashore, round the lower slopes of Barra hill and in a straight line of houses connecting the temple with the community well, a street which became known quite simply and logically as Macao Street. The well—in Portuguese the Poço de Lilau—was called Grandmother's Well in Fukienese, in allusion to Ma Cho, the patroness and saviour, and it became the new city's first and oldest well, used by Portuguese and Fukienese alike.

The presence of an able and industrious Fukienese community as neighbours assured the Portuguese of good fish supplies and plenty of fresh water, and equally important, a ready source of skilled carpenters, boatbuilders, and ship repairers. The construction of Fukienese ships, with their marked curvature, had numerous features in common with the great Portuguese ships of the day, and Fukienese ship carpenters evidently had little difficulty in adapting themselves to European methods of construction and repair. From this there developed from the start a community of interest between the two races, and in the years that followed the Fukienese held a special place in Macao society, being exempt from a number of rules and restrictions imposed on other Chinese. As the subsequent expansion and development of the Ma Cho Temple demonstrates, the community benefited enormously from the Portuguese presence in Macao. Within fifty years they had become the principal shipbuilders and repairers for the whole of the Pearl River estuary, a very large area.

Symptomatic of how little anything changes, the descendants of the community still live in this southern part of Macao, in which Fukienese is widely spoken, with Cantonese of course as the *lingua franca*.

Within a short time, Cantonese farmers were attracted to nearby parts of Heungshan district, the rural population of which in the following decades rose steadily, basing its livelihood on supplying Macao with pigs, fowl, eggs, and vegetables. A few Cantonese farmers learnt to cater for Western requirements by milking cows and making butter, two activities foreign to South China.

Building started along the waterfront of the inner harbour. With a small population and plenty of land, a tradition of large houses and gardens began from the start, gardens being surrounded by high walls as protection from the winds. Trade went for the low, riverine sites, religion for the hills. On the flourishing Japan trade the city grew rapidly. Private houses were cool and spacious, with shutters instead of glass to keep out sun and rain, and with simple colonnaded verandahs on which to sit out comfortably in the breeze. Later, windows were added behind the shutters, with latticed windowpanes of shell.

By 1565 there were two churches, the one maintained by the Jesuits holding 300 people, and more religious buildings and private houses were going up all the time. There was no question of which was the more important, religion or trade. Each was the concern of a different set of people, and Macao accommodated both. As the city developed as an entrepôt, so it did as a religious centre. On the one hand it was attracting trade. On the other it was sending out missionaries to every country in the Far East.

Chinese moves to curb Macao's liberty—ground rent

The extraordinary freedom the city enjoyed in its very early days—freedom from the restrictions both of China and of the Portuguese authorities at Goa and Malacca—was too good to last. The prosperity of the budding city soon became a commercial threat to Canton. The Kwangtung provincial revenue was affected, and so too were the perquisites of officials, since Chinese merchants avoided these levies, licit and illicit, by transacting their business at Macao. It was decided in Canton that more effective measures were needed to bring the foreign city within the framework of proper Chinese control.

In 1573, at the narrowest point of the peninsula, about a mile north of the settlement, a Chinese customs barrier was set up to levy dues on goods passing in and out. This was only partially effective, a large part of the traffic being water-borne up the devious channels of the delta. In 1578 twice-yearly trade fairs were started in Canton, which the Portuguese had permission to attend. This established a better division of trade between the two cities. It also kept foreign trade more under the eye of the senior provincial authorities, who were thus assured of a proper collection of revenue and perquisites.

The presentation of gifts to officials in China was sanctioned by long custom. It would have been impolite for the Portuguese not to have given presents to the officials in contact with Macao. As the presents were often valuable and novel, and still more often in cash, they were keenly sought after, with results that worsened. By refusing—or at first withholding consent to—a request, by picking on a technical offence and magnifying its importance, or by merely threatening something undesirable, the Heungshan magistrate, in whose juridical area Macao lay, and the Canton officers in charge of trade and shipping, could provoke splendid gifts to themselves. The Portuguese had no means of knowing whether the orders and threats issued to them were imperial, gubernatorial, or merely out of the magistrate's own head; and being an immensely wealthy community, they found it simpler to give than to argue.

Certain gifts regularly made eventually assumed the nature of a tax. Of such, the most important was the ground rent that from this time (1578) had to be paid for the area the Portuguese occupied. This, originally a personal gift, ended as an item of revenue insisted upon by the Chinese authorities, and invoked in later generations to prove that the Portuguese had never been granted sovereign rights.

While Macao remained rich and prosperous, these Chinese exactions were of small import. Not till later, when the Portuguese fell on harder times, did their true restrictive nature become apparent. By that time, so far as the Chinese were concerned, they were sanctioned by long custom, while on the Portuguese side no one could remember how or why they had begun in the first place.

Macao in 1600

The great Portuguese epoch in Asia lasted for about ninety years, from the capture of Goa in 1510 to the arrival of the Dutch at the end of the century. Macao's golden epoch, resting on the Japan trade, lasted from the settlement's foundation in 1557, to the end of the Japan trade and the fall of Malacca, in 1641. In 1600, when Portuguese Asia, strangely independent of Portugal, and as much an Asian trading organization as a European one, was fatally threatened by the Dutch, Macao was at its zenith.

Of all the cities of the Far East influenced architecturally by Europe, Macao was the finest. Trees had grown up on the two southern hills of Barra and Penha; high-walled gardens surrounded the few large houses and churches on the Ridge, the gentle slope separating the two harbours. Around the bay of the outer harbour, the Praia Grande was lined with well-built stone houses. Approached from the open sea, this long crescent of buildings, with squat towers and low domes of classical churches rising behind them, so gave the place the appearance of a Mediterranean city that it was difficult to imagine oneself in China. There was scarcely a street without a church, and crowning everything, on the slope of the most central and prominent hill, rose the seminary of the Jesuits, the university where missionaries were trained for service throughout the Far East, for China, Japan, Korea, the Indo-Chinese states, Siam, and Borneo.

The old fort of Monte today stands on part of this site, but in 1600 the whole of Macao was unfortified. The seminary extended down the hill on the west side, where there were other buildings and a large garden, in which experiments were carried out in transplanting foreign vegetables and herbs used in medicine, and where Chinese medicinal plants were cultivated and studied. Lower on the hillside, adjoining the seminary garden and buildings, was the city's most splendid religious building, the Jesuit church of São Paulo, built entirely of wood gracefully carved, completed in 1602.

Peter Mundy, who saw it some years later, was profoundly impressed. 'The rooffe is of the fairest Arche that yet I ever saw to my remembrance,' he wrote, 'of excellentt worckemanshippe, Carved in wood, curiously guilt and painted with exquisite collours.' The roof was apparently contrived in descending whorls of wood, splendidly carved and painted, gold being the predominant element in the general decoration of the interior. It must have been about the most sumptuous church in Asia.

The stone facade, which is all that survives of the church today, was added between 1633 and 1635, erected with the help of the Jesuits' Japanese students and converts.

Looking out across the Chinese countryside from Macao, it might be thought that Portugal had had no influence on China whatever. In fact, even by 1600 Portuguese influence on China was already considerable, albeit invisible other than to the trained eye. Mainly it was an influence on diet.

Although milk and butter did not find favour with the Cantonese, there was an extensive dietary interchange.

Numerous foreign vegetables were introduced from Macao into China. Some of them were cultivated only in Heungshan for Macao's consumption, but others found their way into the Cantonese cuisine, and thus to other parts of China.

Sweet potatoes and peanuts were the two most important—one of the most significant results of the entire European connexion with China. The cultivation of sweet potatoes, grown as a winter crop in practically every South China village today, greatly strengthened village economy, while peanuts provided the oil in which today the greater part of all Chinese cooking is done.

Among the other vegetables introduced were green beans, sprouts, and lettuce. Watercress is still called in Cantonese the Western Ocean vegetable, the Western Ocean being the colloquial name for Portugal. Pineapples, guavas, papayas, custard apples (foreign devils' laichee), and chillies were also brought by the Portuguese from other parts of their widely-scattered empire. Another important innovation of theirs was the making of shrimp paste (*ham ha*), which has become a sideline industry of even the remotest villages along the South China coast.

In the opposite direction, from China to the West, via Macao, came rhubarb, celery, tea, and the delicious dwarf oranges—*kat*—that grow in the delta villages and which, transplanted to Tangier, then under Portuguese control, became known in Europe as tangerines.

Another significant, though lesser-known, item was the export of Chinese boars for cross-breeding with the European pig, in those days a sorry animal, and which led ultimately to raised standards of pork over most of Western Europe.

Then, further up the river, out of sight of Macao but easily accessible through the delta, was the low-priced, non-luxury silk industry inaugurated and managed by the women of

Shuntak district. This began as a direct outcome of Macao's outlet to Japan, brought silk within the purchasing power of millions who would not otherwise be able to afford it, and made Shuntak one of the wealthiest districts in South China.

There were no shops in Macao, nor were there till well into the nineteenth century. When wines, dried foodstuffs, and other non-perishables arrived from Europe, word quickly went round, and one purchased in bulk from the shipper or his agent. As a result, each house needed a large amount of storage space. This was one of the reasons why families lived in the upper floors of their houses, leaving the ground floor rooms sparsely furnished, to be used for storage when required.

Chinese, unless they were Christians, were not allowed to sleep the night in the city. This was insisted on by Chinese and Portuguese authorities alike. Christian Chinese were not itemized as being excluded from the Chinese rule, but in practice they were. When a Chinese became Christian, he cut his hair in the prevailing Western way and often wore European clothes. Chinese coiffure for men in the Ming dynasty consisted of shaving the upper part of the forehead to give the impression of a high brow, letting the rest of the hair grow long, drawn back into a twisted knot secured by pins of jade or bamboo. Once a Chinese abandoned his traditional hair-style, no further attention was paid to him by his country's officials. In an indefinable way he ceased to be Chinese.

The day population was thus higher than the night population. At dusk, Chinese labourers, stonecutters and masons, market gardeners, petty merchants and hawkers who made their living in Macao, wended their way back through the fields north of the town, past the customs barrier and out to their villages, leaving Macao with between 5,000 and 6,000 residents.

Of these it is thought that about 1,000 were Portuguese. The richer ones had so much wealth that it needed a fertile imagination to know what to do with it. Nearby farms produced everything needed for their tables, to which the city added imported Portuguese wines and the delicious sweetmeats that are a feature of Macao's cuisine. With cut glass from Europe, and vessels, plates, and candle-sticks of Indian silver from Goa, a dinner was a fine affair. Yet for all their wealth, Macao men newly returned from a voyage would walk barefoot to their churches to give thanks for their safe home-coming, and offer thanksgiving money to the patron saints.

The marriage problem

There were no Portuguese women in Macao, and very few anywhere in Asia. Men therefore followed the custom set in the older settlements of marrying Asian girls, provided they were Christians, or became so on marriage. In the first ten years of Macao's existence, due to a total lack of Chinese Christians, wives ranked as a significant item in the list of imports.

They were primarily sought from Malacca, which after forty-five years of Portuguese occupancy had a large mixed-race Christian population, of which Macao could be seen as a celibate extension, with affinities closer to Malacca than anywhere else.

Another source of wives was Japan. Nagasaki, growing from a fishing village to a large town on the wealth of the Portuguese trade, had a resident Portuguese community. Despite St Francis Xavier's disappointing conclusions about conversion in Japan, the Jesuits continued to peg away, and with mounting success. As their conversions increased, Portuguese men married Japanese Christian girls. Some of these new families had connexions with Macao, where Japanese Christians engaged in the trade found it convenient to install their relatives as agents. A small Japanese community was thus an early feature of

Macao, where of course more Luso-Japanese weddings took place.

From these three main strands—Portuguese, Malacca mestiça, and Japanese—the native-born Macanese originated. After the first ten or twenty years a Chinese strain was added. Among the poorer class of Chinese of whom the Portuguese had experience, girls were often unwanted children, the lore of China being that a girl has to be fed and clothed for fifteen years or so, yet to no profit, since on marriage she goes to her husband's family, depriving her own of a pair of hands. The treatment girls received in China so shocked the Portuguese that it became a charitable act to adopt Chinese infant girls, bringing them up as Christians. As these girls grew up, a new supply for marriages was created.

Though the mestiça wives were by and large europeanized, they still retained their Malacca custom of concealing their faces in public. This they did by means of a light shawl thrown loosely over the head and held with one hand, so that when men were passing it could be drawn quickly across the face.

Sarong and cabaia, the distinctive women's tunic that originated in Portuguese Malacca, was the commonest women's attire. Even the Japanese wives wore sarong and cabaia when going out, though on returning home they changed into kimono. Women's shoes were soled and heeled in cork, from Portugal. It is a small indication of the wealth of the community that material for women's shoes came from the other side of the world.

In the streets, women either walked or were carried in norimons, Japanese litters similar to a bowl-shaped tray with a handle each end, through which passed an ornamented rod shaped like a cupid's bow, borne on the shoulders of two slaves. Men who could afford it rode out on horseback, grazing their horses in the fields between the town and the customs barrier.

The slave population more than doubled the Portuguese community, each family keeping several slaves. Africans, Indians, and Malays, each came from one of the Portuguese possessions. Their varied appearance and costume demonstrated the extent and variety of the lands influenced by Portugal.

People prided themselves on the fine apparel of their slaves, and it was not uncommon to find them clad in damask. African slaves, in the hope of bettering themselves, sometimes ran away into China. Eventually there came to be quite a community of them in one of the suburbs of Canton. Merchants engaged in foreign trade sometimes used them as interpreters.

When Peter Mundy was entertained in Macao, music was played during dinner, though he said it was only 'indifferent good'. Unlike Goa, no indigenous musical tradition developed, mainly due to Chinese being uninterested in European music. The best music was connected with the Church. The Jesuits had what amounted to a faculty of music in their seminary, and it was evidently of a high order. Japanese were among their best pupils.

Macao in its heyday differed from other Portuguese establishments in its standards. There was a liberalness, a moderation, which set it in a class apart. In Macao the Portuguese never went wild with wealth, as they often did elsewhere. This was partly because of being governed by the Senate, rather than by corrupt and venal officials from Goa, and partly because of the neighbouring but presiding influence of the Chinese mandarinate, which made a man think twice before committing excesses that might rebound not just on himself but on the whole town.

The Macanese were not confined to their peninsula. Across the inner harbour, on the hilly island of Lappa, the religious orders and wealthier citizens had farms and country houses, a favourite occupation being to shoot quail and other wild fowl over the lonely, grass-covered hills. No Portuguese, however poor, engaged in any form of manual labour, the community being strictly a trading one.

Christianity's setback in Japan

Religious missions in the East operated under a working arrangement introduced by Rome and known in Portuguese as the *padroado*, or patronage. This, loosely defined, decreed that all Catholic missionaries, of whatever nationality, working in the Portuguese sphere of influence must have the approval of the King of Portual and sail East under his auspices. China, Japan, and mainland Asia were included in Portugal's *padroado*; the Philippines came to be included in Spain's. Macao was the seat of padroado Jesuits, while Manila, which quickly grew into a missionary centre as important as Macao, was from 1577 the headquarters of the Franciscans. Augustinians worked in both patronages, but had less political influence than these other Orders.

The Franciscans, whose activities were thus in effect confined to the Philippines, soon began showing signs of restiveness with these arrangements, and started 'poaching' in Jesuits areas, with results of which they did not foresee the gravity.

While Christianity and trade flourished in Japan, all went well for Macao. By 1582 there were estimated to be 150,000 Japanese Christians. But in 1587 the Japanese shogun Hideyoshi, autocrat ruler of Japan from 1582 to 1598, apprehensive lest the growing power of the new faith be put to political use, issued an edict expelling all missionaries from the country.

The edict was not acted upon at once. The Jesuits continued their work more privately, and Christianity might still have prospered had not a group of Spanish Franciscans, arriving a few years later from Manila, flouted the Japanese government by preaching and converting openly. In their determination to out-do the Jesuits, whom they foolishly regarded as rivals, they did irreparable harm to the Christian cause, revealing to the Japanese the national rifts within the Church, and the political danger that might result for Japan if she associated herself with any one group.

The completing touch came in 1596, when a shipwrecked Spanish pilot, in altercation with a minor Japanese ruler, boasted of Spanish power, informing him that Spain was not just a nation of missionaries and traders; these were merely the advance guard, preparing the way for military forces to come.

Report of this encounter, delivered to Hideyoshi, confirmed his suspicions. The anti-Christian edict was re-issued. Several Spanish Franciscans and a number of their Japanese converts were crucified at Nagasaki, beginning a spasmodic, but eventually general, persecution of Christians throughout Japan. Christian Japanese who could afford to, or had the opportunity, started leaving the country. Many of them came to Macao. At first they were of the poorer sort, servants and others assisted by Portuguese residents in Nagasaki. Later came more educated people, fleeting from a suppression that proved to be one of the most ruthless in the entire history of Christianity.

But the masks of tragedy and comedy always hang side by side. As if there were not already enough celibates in Macao, Portuguese bachelors from India and Malacca were coming there on the look-out for dowries from magnates in the Japan trade. The arrival of Japanese refugee families caused a providential increase in the number of Macao's marriageable girls, at a time when demand was unexpectedly keen.

The four seasons of Macao's fabulous prosperity
Trade followed the seasons. In early summer, the Japan fleet came up from Malacca. May and June are months of humid

heat and heavy rainfall in Macao, and shifting cargoes was troublesome, the brown waters of the inner harbour lashed angrily by rain. As soon as possible the fleet left for Japan, since the later the departure the greater the risk of meeting a typhoon, the season for which occurs between July and October. With an early start and good fortune, the ships could catch one of the fair periods with which the summer rains are interspersed, making the entire voyage to Nagasaki in good weather. If they were delayed loading cargo, they would generally stay at Macao till the following summer.

During the fleet's absence, the summer trade fair took place in Canton, lasting several weeks, during which produce from the Spice Islands, India, Europe, and the Middle East was exchanged for Chinese goods. By November, the hot uncertain summer was replaced by the pleasantest season of the year; and by Christmas, with untroubled seas and the wind blowing steadily from the north, the fleet returned from Nagasaki. At Macao, the ships off-loaded some of the Japanese silver, loaded goods from Canton, and sailed for Malacca early in the new year. During the winter, another fair was held at Canton, and soon the wet summer wind began blowing from the south, the rains started, and with them the same process over again.

From Malacca to Macao, the holds contained cargoes partly for China and partly for Japan. Those for China included always a large consignment of pepper and other seasonings from the Moluccas (obtained at the risk of a fight with the Spaniards, and later with the Dutch), high-quality cotton and muslin from India, from Europe a variety of things including metalware, cut glass, mirrors, clocks, and wine, and from the Middle East jewellery, daggers, and a diversity of bric-à-brac. Lesser though no less valuable items included edible birds'-nests from Siam, and cockatoos from Macassar, esteemed because they could be taught to talk.

At Macao, the principal cargo for Japan was loaded: Chinese silk, raw and prepared, the demand for which was so great in Japan that merchants at Macao thought nothing of making a 200% profit on every consignment. In earlier years profits had been even higher, the very first silk cargoes being sold at twelve times their value. Bric-à-brac sold well in Japan; so did firearms, daggers, Persian carpets, battle pictures, and other works of art. Staple imports included Indian cotton, spices, and European wines.

The Portuguese ships returned from Nagasaki, after their tremendous sales, with hundreds of thousands of cruzados' worth of silver aboard. This treasure could in its turn be sold on the fluctuating silver market of Canton, to even further advantage. With it, Macao merchants bought Chinese goods for delivery westward to India and Europe. Three or four successful private voyages between Macao and Nagasaki could mean retirement to Europe with a fortune. Only the danger of the seas, the possibility of making more, and the pleasantness of Macao itself, kept the population as stable as it was.

Trade in the official fleet was a royal preserve, but as explained earlier, there were accepted methods of infringing this. Macao private vessels sailed with the fleet for protection, and those Macanese not wealthy enough to own a ship, or buy a suitable gift for the Captain-Major for permission to sail in one of the royal ships, could always send their goods in the care of someone else, for sale on commission. If everyone in Macao could not afford a good-sized bite, they could all at least nibble; and when the fleet sailed out into the estuary, and headed for the rising sun, it bore with it the investments and hopes of nearly everyone in the city. 'Even the humblest citizens could make little fortunes, at times.'

On the return journey, from Macao to Malacca, went a certain amount of Japanese silver, and later copper; but the bulk of the cargo was Chinese. Silk predominated—delicately woven embroideries and brocades; seed pearls—there were oyster-beds in the shallow bays of the Pearl River; musk, ginger, medicinal drugs, gold and lead; porcelain, then at a high standard of decorativeness and quality, and already including articles produced exclusively for the Western market, such as tea-cups with handles, jugs and flat dishes not normally used in China; and lastly rhubarb, a vegetable so much in demand in Europe that Cantonese wiseacres believed that Europeans, a constipated race, would die if the supply stopped.

In addition to this great trade route, there were several local routes operated by lesser merchants and by Chinese. Most important was that to the rising city of Manila, capital of the Philippines. Chinese Christians in both cities played a prominent part here. For the Portuguese, though since 1580 the crowns of Spain and Portugal had been united, Spanish Manila was a rival city; and though there were Spaniards resident at Macao, and some Portuguese in Manila, there was little love lost between them.

The basement Chinese

As regards Chinese, while forbidden to reside at Macao, they performed many duties essential to the Macanese, as personal servants, laundrymen, hawkers from whom one purchased the best fruits and freshest vegetables, wharf labourers, barbers, and other humble services. As these were constantly needed, it was inconvenient to have the Cantonese population leaving for the district every evening, and various Macanese, in defiance of the law, allowed them to say in the basement of their houses. The Chinese genius for compromise was infectious. How could it be said of people living in basements that they were seeking permanent residence? The Senate accepted this bland reasoning. Its members found the nightly departure of Chinese as tiresome as everyone else did. Accordingly, Chinese occupied basements, where they prospered and multiplied.

Nor was every one of them a menial, although such was the fiction officially maintained. Some of them were businessmen trading to Manila and elsewhere, with their own junks, and with relatives in foreign ports. The district officials of Heungshan, informed of this, used it as one of their standard means of provoking gifts, the 'seizure' of infant Chinese girls and employment of Japanese and African servants being others, all of which recurred at intervals, whenever Macao was tardy or parsimonious with its presents. Of course, if a Chinese merchant chose to become Christian, he escaped both the attentions of Heungshan officialdom and confinement to a basement. These were advantages some Cantonese merchants were quick to appreciate.

A blind eye was turned on the resident Fukien community because they were boatbuilders, thus vital to the city's existence. Another Cantonese method of avoiding basement life was to do a deal with a Fukienese and become a boatbuilder, though without building boats.

Thus Macao in the days of its greatness: a city of adventurers enjoying a rich life, confidently aware that at any moment they might have to fight for it. Bold and superstitious, hospitable and remarkably tolerant of outsiders who came in peace, kind to each other, with a strong sense of being one community, they conducted their trade and worshipped in their churches, with their golden-skinned Malacca wives and sun-blackened African slaves, their entire lives the unique, exotic fruit of the grafting of West on East.

4

Dutch Assaults on Macao

Union of the Crowns—Dutch and English in Asian trade
Portuguese Asia had proved itself strong enough to hold the
Spaniards in check in Eastern waters. It was not to prove strong
enough against the Dutch. Just as the Spanish penetration into
Asia stems from the predilections of one man—the dissatisfied
Magellan—so does the disaster to which Portugal and her
empire were now to be submitted stem from the dreams and
predilections of another individual—in this case a king.

In 1578 this young king, Sebastião, imbued with a fantastic
and fatal desire for glory, which the heroic tone of Camões'
epic is said partly to have inspired or aggravated, led a large
but ill-prepared army, with a baggage train staggering in its
opulence and unwieldiness, against the Muslims in North Africa.
In the desert near Alcâcer-Quebir he imprudently advanced upon
a Muslim host vastly outnumbering his own. The battle lasted
an hour, at the end of which the flower of Portugal's manhood
lay dead on the burning sand, the body of their king lost among
them, unrecognizable.

A catastrophic figure, Sebastião belonged to the age of
chivalry, but was born two centuries too late. As ruler of a
commercial state, he would have been wiser to have occupied
himself with the price of pepper and nutmeg, or with the more
light-hearted but no less important problem of getting married
and producing children. For he died without an heir. He was
succeeded by his aged great-uncle, Dom Henrique, who was a
Cardinal, and who succumbed a few months later, leaving the
way open for Philip II of Spain, one of the possible heirs, to
claim the crown of Portugal, a union with Spain which brought

about the downfall of the Portuguese empire in Asia, and narrowly missed expunging Portugal's identity as a separate state. A Spanish army invaded Portugal in support of Philip's pretensions, and in December 1580 Philip himself crossed the frontier. Portugal ceased to be an independent nation.

It was some time before Lisbon felt the disastrous outcome of the Union of the Crowns. Philip II was courteous. The kingdom of Portugal, together with its overseas possession, was to be administered separately from Spain. A council of Portuguese notables would reside at Madrid, all matters concerning Portugal being dealt with through them.

But after the failure of the Spanish Armada in 1588, the crippling nature of the union took effect. Obsessed with his hatred of Elizabethan England, Philip ordered the closure of Portuguese ports, as well as Spanish, to English shipping, thus making Portugal party to Anglo-Spanish enmity. For Elizabeth I it was no displeasure to authorize attacks on the rich Portuguese carracks from the Indies. When one of them, the *Madre de Deus*, was captured in 1591 off the Azores and brought back to Plymouth, it created a popular sensation. The ship was reckoned the largest ever seen. People came from miles to gape at her. Shipwrights examined her—and learnt.

A few years later, in 1594, disorders in the Spanish Netherlands resulted in the same closure of ports being applied to the Dutch. Hitherto, both Dutch and English had been able to trade in oriental wares in Portuguese ports. Had these ports remained open, Portugal might have maintained for much longer her position as intermediary in Eastern commerce. Closure, meaning the loss of a valuable trade, served as an irritant arousing the dynamic energy of the Dutch and the English to go, as the Portuguese had done, to the sources of supply.

In 1595 the first Dutch fleet, guided by Jan Huyghen van Linschoten, a Dutch resident of Lisbon who knew the route to

India, set off for Java. In 1601, under charter from Queen Elizabeth, a company of London merchants, predecessors of the Honourable East India Company, sent their first ship to the Spice Islands. The following year, the Netherlands East India Company was formed.

The viceregal government at Goa did what it could to meet the new situation, but Philip III (1598–1621) was naturally more interested in safeguarding colonies founded by Spanish efforts and money than in answering Portuguese pleas for reinforcements. While the English began modestly, sending an envoy to the Mughal Emperor Jehangir, and obtaining permission to have small trading places on the west coast of India, the Dutch, in a systematic penetration of the Indies supported by military force, swept the Portuguese out of their hard-earned possessions, and laid the outlines of what became the Dutch East Indies. From their base in Java, they attempted to wrest the Japan trade out of Portuguese hands, menacing ships passing round the foot of the Malay peninsula on their way between Malacca and Macao.

Fortification—Dutch in Japan

In 1601 Dutch sails were sighted off Macao for the first time. Amazed to find the city unfortified, the Dutch sent two men ashore as spokesmen, while another party attempted to take soundings in the harbour. The Macanese, fully informed of the hostile Dutch venture in the Indies, deemed the answer to be severity. They set upon the sounding party, capturing most of them after a sharp fight. Eighteen were publicly hanged.

The Dutch ships withdrew; but as Macao realized, this was only a first essay. The Hollanders, with their native thoroughness and determination, with good armament and the full backing of their government, would not be prepared to concede victory after a skirmish. After other Dutch fleets had appeared in two successive years, each time doing some damage, it was decided that defences must be erected round the seaward edge of the peninsula.

Begun in 1606, the defensive works caused a major excitement among the Cantonese in Macao, large numbers of whom fled to the district. A rumour that Father Cataneo, at the Jesuit seminary, was preparing to lead a military expedition into China to seize the throne—he wore Chinese clothes—gained a credence widened by the complete ignorance of educated Chinese about anything to do with Christianity, or indeed with the outside world. A young Jesuit missionary working in Kwangtung was tortured to death in an attempt to gain information about the projected invasion, and it was not until a Chinese military officer was sent to inspect the seminary, and meet the supposed pretender to the throne, that the scare subsided, Cantonese workers returned, and life went back to normal.

The incident, however, served the Chinese as an excuse for making more restrictive rules. It was decreed that in future all new buildings in Macao must have a permit from the Heungshan authorities. Ships, too, were only to be repaired under licence, and must not exceed a certain tonnage. These orders, which with modifications prevailed until the nineteenth century, were not always respected, but they provided new methods of provoking gifts for magisterial purses.

In 1607 the Portuguese engaged a Dutch fleet off Lantao Island, and drove it off to sea. In the following year they learnt from their own fleet returning from Japan that the Dutch had succeeded in securing a base on the island of Hirado, not far from Nagasaki. To operate between there and Java, now more fully under Dutch influence, they were proposing to establish a post on Formosa, which now became their sheltering and revictualling point on the Japan route.

There followed a twelve-year period of truce between the Netherlands and Spain (including Portugal)—the Truce of Antwerp, signed in 1609—but in the East this did not end Luso-Dutch enmity, or prevent continued Dutch chiselling into Portugal's trade system. During the truce years, Macao wisely proceeded with its programme of fortification, in preparation for the next onslaught. Forts were built on Barra hill, the southernmost point of Macao commanding entry to the inner harbour, and at each end of the Praia Grande commanding the outer harbour.

Even the Jesuits took part in the defensive preparations. That part of their buildings and garden that occupied the top of the Monte disappeared for ever from view behind a great square of fortress walls, still there to this day, through which a concealed passage led to the adjacent college and church of São Paulo. A gun foundry was set up under Manuel Bocarro, whose products, the finest of their kind throughout Asia, played an unobserved though telling part in the transformation of war in the Far East, his cannon being at various times sold to all the neighbouring countries.

The Dutch invasion

The Dutch quickly found that profit in the Japan trade depended on the availability of Chinese silk, for which Macao held the monopoly and Japan's demand was insatiable. On Formosa silk could only be obtained, at irregular intervals and subject to much hard bargaining, from Chinese pirates. Among the Dutch, a section of opinion loudly favoured attempting the capture of Macao.

The Truce of Antwerp had not expired more than a few months before a Dutch fleet under Cornelis van Reijersen approached Macao. English ships were also in the fleet, but the English had a more pacific policy than the Dutch in the East, and in what followed the English played no part. Reijersen was one of those who advocated seizing Macao, and although his orders did not specifically detail him to attack it, he thought he would take the chance.

It was June 1622. The Japan fleet had got in from Malacca some days earlier, but most of the Macao Portuguese were abroad in various parts of the Far East. A number of men had responded to a recent request by the King of Siam for soldiers for his bodyguard, and left for Ayuthia. Another group was somewhere in China, having gone by agreement with the Imperial Government to assist in the defence of the North against the Manchus, who were beginning the series of attacks which twenty-two years later led to the fall of the Ming dynasty. When the Dutch force appeared, there were not more than 1,000 people in the city, with only eighty Europeans capable of bearing arms.

The engagement began on 23rd June, when the Dutch tried to enter the outer harbour by bombarding the forts defending it. After an all-day fight, they retired with the loss of one ship. Next day, St John the Baptist's Day, they resumed the bombardment, though this time as a feint. Simultaneously, they landed their main force near Cacilhas Bay, on a beach defended only by a hastily-dug sandbank, at the north-east end of the peninsula. From there, meeting only light opposition, they advanced through the fields towards the edge of the city, on its undefended side.

Every man, lay and cleric, free and slave, rose to the defence. The Jesuits quickly shifted guns to the north side of their fortress-seminary. Dealing with the Peking Court, to which gifts of cannon were most acceptable, the Jesuits were adept in gunnery. There were precious few guns or men to fire them on this occasion, and nothing like a steady cannonade could be brought upon the advancing Dutch force, but this deficiency was compensated for by good marksmanship. As the enemy approached the lower slopes of the Monte, Father Rho scored a direct hit on the main Dutch powder magazine, which blew up with a tremendous explosion.

Even after this loss, the Dutch continued to press their attack; but being short of ammunition, and unaware of the perilously small size of the force defying them, they hesitated at the main entry into the city, between the hills of Monte and Guia. They were preparing to advance to take one of these hills and secure themselves, when Portuguese reinforcements arrived from the outer harbour forts, the defenders on that side having realized that the Dutch did not intend landing on the Praia Grande.

This unexpected increase in strength gave the Portuguese a sudden *élan* of confidence. The nation's battle cry— 'St Iago!'—rang out from somewhere, and was a second later being yelled from every throat as the diminutive force, each man like one inspired, charged down from all sides upon the Dutch. Their onrush, after several hours of defensive action, confused their adversaries, making them uncertain how the battle was going, for the Portuguese were attacking with the fury and enthusiasm of those who believe themselves victorious. Under cover of all the fire they could muster, the foremost of the Portuguese closed with the enemy to engage him hand to hand.

The impact of their advance was decisive. The Dutch commanding officer was among the first to fall. As they lost sight of him, the invaders wavered. A moment later they were retreating in disorder to their boats. Chasing them through the fields, the Macanese threw away their firearms and slew the Dutch with their swords. An African woman dressed as a man even killed two Dutchmen with a prong.

The rout was joined by the entire population, Jesuits included. Many Hollanders were killed, others taken prisoner, and several drowned while trying to reach the boats. It could not have been a more complete victory. On the following day, the Dutch sent ships flying a truce flag to ask for the ransom of prisoners. This being refused, they sailed away. In the rejoicings that followed, many slaves were liberated for their parts in the fighting, and it was decided that every year on St John the Baptist's Day the event should be commemorated with thanksgiving.

The Governor of Kwangtung sent a message of congratulation to the Senate, and a gift of 400 piculs of rice for the negro slaves, who the Governor understood had particularly distinguished themselves.

The city's first Captain-General

Walls were now built along the northern boundary of the city, and urgent requests were made to Goa for a permanent military establishment to supersede the amateur levies which had so far sufficed for protection. By the following year—1623—the position had improved. The men sent to China returned without having been allowed to reach the northern frontier, and a contingent of regular troops was sent from Manila, the first and last benefit Macao derived from the Union of the Crowns.

The other protective step taken by Goa was not so appreciated. A Captain-General of Macao was appointed, and sent from Goa. Though the appointment elevated the city to the same status as Malacca within the framework of the Portuguese empire, it also meant the posting of officialdom within the stronghold of Macao's closely guarded independence. It was in this later aspect that it was viewed by the Macanese, who gave the new appointee neither welcome, cooperation, nor even accommodation.

Had the official chosen been a tactful, moderate person, an understanding might have been reached, though it would have been difficult, for Macao had no intention of giving in. But Dom Francisco Mascarenhas was an authoritarian—he was also seen as a running dog of Spain—and was exceedingly indignant at the cold reception Macao gave him. Eyeing the fortress-seminary, and concluding from its commanding site that it was the seat of opposition, he was only deterred from occupying it when three warning cannon balls were fired at him, a message more succinct than any of the Senate could have composed on paper. Few administrators can have had so strange an arrival in a supposedly loyal territory.

There being no official residence for him, Mascarenhas retired to the Augustinian hermitage—neutral territory—and bided his time. An invitation from the Jesuits to dine at the seminary soon provided him with what he wanted. Accepting, he stayed late, walking in the garden with the fathers until the bell rang calling them to prayers. Surrounded by his armed retinue, he then informed the fathers in the King's name that they had his permission to go and say their prayers, but not to return. The main gates were closed, the unfortunate Jesuits were despatched by the concealed passage to their college and church, and Monte fort became the Captain-General's residence.

More high-handed actions of this kind took place, arousing protests and dissatisfaction on all sides. Within a few months the tensions in the city had become so serious that there was rioting, Mascarenhas' life was threatened, and he finally took refuge aboard ship. When at last he left Macao, there were many who would have liked to have seen the post abolished, but a succession followed, one as unpopular as another, all of them Portuguese appointed by Spain, each receiving no more than minimal respect from the untamed Senate and people.

The last serious Dutch attack took place in 1627, on which occasion a Dutch fleet was routed by Portuguese naval force under Tomas Vieira, a local-born Macanese. Thereafter the

Dutch resigned themselves to collaborating with Chinese pirates to obtain silk, and in effect became pirates themselves, preying upon ships in the straits between Formosa and the Chinese mainland. Their illegally procured or pirated goods were then brought to Formosa, where they joined the cargoes of Dutch ships engaged in legitimate trade between Japan and the Indies.

5

The Passing of Macao's Golden Epoch

The first Britons in China

Among the crews of Portuguese ships sailing to the East were men from the British Isles, opportunists, miscreants, persecuted Catholics, and plain adventurers, all drawn to the wealth and prospects which for a short time were centred in Lisbon. The Portuguese adventure in Asia had an unusually cosmopolitan side to it. We have already observed an Italian, Raffaelo Perestrello, commanding a Portuguese voyage to China. It was the same throughout. Provided a man spoke Portuguese and was a Catholic—or pretended to be—it was not too difficult to find a place for himself in Portuguese Asia.

These early Britishers in the Far East are not easy to trace, one of the reasons being that many of them took Portuguese names, and in old records are not distinguishable as Britons; but of at least one there is fairly substantial record, and as his life gives an idea of what was possible in those times, it will be worth taking a passing glance at it.

In 1579, nine years before the Spanish Armada, a Scottish youth named William Carmichael left his northern shores and reached Lisbon, where he spent two years studying Portuguese, waiting for an opportunity to obtain a berth in an eastward-bound ship. They were critically bad years. The disaster of Alcâcer-Quebir had taken place the year previously, Lisbon was plague-stricken and in a state of crisis created by the impending threat of the Union of the Crowns. Carmichael was in fact still residing in Lisbon when Philip II of Spain came from Madrid to accept his newly acquired kingdom.

The following year—1581—William Carmichael succeeded in getting aboard a ship sailing to Goa, where instead of going into private trade, as must surely have been his original intention, he was engaged by the viceregal government, in the service of which he spent the next thirty years, a remarkable instance of the kind of opportunities which opened out in the Portuguese empire to foreigners who were trusted. At some period during his thirty years' service Carmichael came to the Far East, from which fact it can be said for certain that he visited Macao. He is the first known Britisher in China, and one of the very few who saw Macao in its heyday.

In 1611, he deserted his post and made his way to Macassar in Celebes, which had been seized from the Portuguese by the Dutch a few years earlier. Why he deserted is a mystery. Perhaps he had learnt—it might have been from the Dutch at Hirado— that the English also were trading in the East Indies, by agreement with Netherlands traders, who allowed them the joint use of some of their stations. He would have heard how at the death of Queen Elizabeth, Scotland's James VI had become lord of the two kingdoms. Perhaps in the desire to hear English spoken again . . .

If he expected to be well received by the Dutch on account of their informal understanding with the English, he soon saw his mistake. Arrested by the Dutch at Macassar on suspicion of being a spy sent to gather geographical and trading information in the Dutch sphere of influence, he was imprisoned for two years, which in the tropics in the conditions of those days was a horrifying experience. After release he went to Bantam in Java, where the Dutch and the English both had settlements. There he found Captain Thomas Best, who having made a voyage to India that contributed to establishing the English at Surat, their first Indian station of any importance, was about to return home in his ship, the *Dragon*. By the only stroke of luck he had after quitting the Portuguese, Carmichael managed to persuade Best to take him with him.

In London, Carmichael tried for several years to obtain compensation from the Netherlands East India Company for its ill-treatment of him in Macassar. But in vain. At last, in 1626, he was admitted poverty-stricken to the Charterhouse, where he presumably spent the rest of his days.

The first Englishwomen in China

The next Britons known to have seen Macao during its golden decades had the misfortune to be there when in the Far East the name of England had become joined to that of the Netherlands as the trade rivals and enemies of Portugal. In 1613 the English joined the Dutch in the Japan trade, setting up a small post on the Japanese island of Hirado. Macao being resolutely closed to them, as it was to the Dutch, Formosa was used by the English as their revictualling point *en route* to Japan.

Relations between the Dutch and the English were confusing and changeable. Broadly speaking, while the Dutch did not object to the English sharing their settlements, they resented the pacific attitude of the English, who were not prepared to secure trade by military force, as were the Dutch, or share in the cost of maintaining Dutch troops in the Indies.

The English trading station in Japan lasted for ten years, after which it closed down as a financial loss. The Hollanders' forceful policy in effect prevented the English from engaging to any extent in Far Eastern trade. The English station in Java was maintained—sometimes against Dutch opposition—after the failure of the station in Japan. But gradually the pattern changed, and it became clear that if English traders had any future in Asia, that future lay not in the Spice Islands or the Far East—where the Dutch set the pace—but in the great sub-continent of India.

England's brief connexion with Japan was undistinguished. The one Englishman of note to come to Japan did so as pilot of a Dutch ship. This was Will Adams, who though unknown in the history of his own country, won himself a remarkable place in the history of Japan as the founder of modern Japanese shipbuilding. In the smallest fishing creek in Japan today will be found rowing boats constructed exactly as they are on the coasts of Sussex and Devon, an outcome of the extraordinary influence of Will Adams.

In 1620, shortly before the closure of the English station at Hirado, the English Company sent Richard Frobisher, a ship carpenter, to repair their ships in Japan. Expecting to do a tour of seven years in the East, Frobisher took with him his wife Joan, their two little sons, and a maidservant named Judith, still only in her early teens. They were shipwrecked off the China coast somewhere between Hainan Island and the Pearl River, but by good fortune got safely ashore; and having rescued their money-chest, they were able to pay a Chinese junkmaster to take them on towards Japan. Passing near Macao, their ship was intercepted by a Portuguese vessel on the look-out for pirates, the Frobishers, their maid, and money being brought under arrest into the city.

Though their reception was not hospitable—they were infringers on what had once been Portugal's monopoly trade with Japan—it was commendably lenient. They were detained under a form of house arrest, being allowed to live in a rented house, paying their own way, while making arrangements for their departure. Under these conditions Frobisher purchased 'two barks'.

But the Portuguese had no intention of allowing the Frobishers to proceed towards Japan. They insisted that Frobisher employ Portuguese masters, who it was explained would be responsible for seeing that the English returned whence they had come—to one of the Dutch stations in Java. There was an obvious risk for the Frobishers in this. Vessels under Portuguese command would not be able to sail to Java in safety, and to say they were going to was merely a polite way of telling Frobisher that he was about to be taken to Portuguese Malacca. As he was at the mercy of the Portuguese, there seemed to him to be no alternative but to take this risk.

Catholic priests who came in touch with the Frobishers, possibly in the capacity of interpreters, understood the danger, and taking pity on the little maidservant Judith, persuaded her to become a Catholic and remain at Macao. The Frobishers, as they feared, were taken in their two barks to Malacca, where they were imprisoned, Frobisher later being killed. In 1625 his widow was repatriated to the English station in Java in exchange for two Portuguese women. There are indications that in accepting repatriation she deserted her two sons. Anyway, within a year she had married again and was in London. She later said her sons died in Malacca.

Joan Frobisher and Judith were the first Englishwomen known to have come to China. Judith, whose name was changed to Julia, entered the orphanage maintained in Macao by the Santa Casa da Misericordia.

This remarkable organization, known wherever Portuguese are to be found, was started by one of the best-loved women in Portugal's history, Queen Leonor, at that time—1498—widow of João II (1484–95). Twelve years after Macao's foundation the Santa Casa was established there (1569), and the record of its activities conveys perhaps better than anything else how far in advance of its times Macao was during its golden epoch. In addition to its orphanage, the Santa Casa ran a leprosarium and a hospital, in which treatment for the indigent was free. It also administered large charitable funds, used for such purposes as providing dowries for orphan girls, and supporting the widows and children of men lost at sea. Nor was it ever short of money. The big traders made and gave handsomely. To be on the board of directors of the Santa Casa was a coveted distinction, and has remained so to this day.

Little Judith—or Julia as she now was—grew up at the orphanage, where she witnessed the Dutch invasion of Macao. At length she received a proposal of marriage from a young Macanese, and became a beneficiary of the Santa Casa's dowry system for orphans. Without a dowry, the only future for a parentless girl was to join a religious order or sink to beggary. In Julia's case, the Santa Casa, instead of providing a dowry of money, secured for her fiancé a post in the customs at Malacca. Soon after her marriage, she travelled south to Malacca with her young husband, and there some years later Peter Mundy met her and noted in his diary 'an Englishwoman Married to a Portugall Mestizo of some quality, are well to live, and have beetweene them one pretty boy.'

In 1641 Malacca fell to the Dutch, but many of the Portuguese community survived, and at Malacca today they are still a distinct community, closely resembling in appearance their Chinese and Malay neighbours, yet preserving still their Catholic religion and Portuguese names. Julia's descendants are perhaps among them.

The first English ship in China—fines and food

We have already seen how Portugal, in the tremendous effort of the Discoveries, overtaxed her strength. Her men were scattered too far, her commitments were too exacting, her population and treasury too small, her ships too few. The Union of the Crowns, with the neglect of Portugal's possessions that it inevitably caused, hastened her decline.

Spain, in what might have been Portugal's interest as well as her own, fought a long rearguard resistance to the Dutch in the

Moluccas, as well as trying to exert influence in Japan, China, Cambodia, Siam, Formosa, and Borneo. None of this activity brought the least profit. By 1640 the power of Spain in the East had found its limits in the waters surrounding the Philippines.

The dynamic nature of Holland's seizure of position was irresistible. Though arriving late on the scene, the Netherlanders captured—and held till 1947—the islands of pepper, cloves, and nutmeg, of which reports and rumours in medieval Europe had set wise men thinking, and started the first voyages of the Navigator. At the end of the Truce of Antwerp, i.e. from 1621 onwards, the Hollanders quickly tidied up their gains in the Indies. By blockading the waters around Singapore (then an obscure fishing village) they made communication between Macao and Malacca so dangerous that the one profitable route left to the Portuguese—the Japan route—was all but completely severed. To add to Portugal's misfortunes, it happened that from 1625 to 1630 England was once more at war with Spain (including Portugal), and English ships had thus every excuse to join the Dutch in their hostilities.

When Charles I of England and Philip IV of Spain made peace in 1630, in the Treaty of Madrid, the power pattern of the colonial era in Asia was forming. Fortified by what they had learned from Portugal and Spain, the Dutch and English were sailing into the East with all the vigour and pioneering spirit that characterized the Portuguese a century earlier. The Portuguese were no match for them. Moreover, with their weakness they had grown timorous. At the Treaty of Madrid they refused to allow English ships and men to frequent Portuguese ports. Peter Mundy, when refused permission to trade at Macao a few years later, in 1637, put his finger on it when he wrote in his diary that the Portuguese considered 'thatt if wee had Free trading here would allsoe trafficke For Japan, and thatt theirby theirs would Decay and soe consequently proove their utter undooing.' The chronicler of the same voyage noted how the famed Japan fleet, last hope of Portuguese Asia, was reduced to only '6 small Vessells'.

Undeterred by Lisbon's refusal to come to terms, William Methwold, President of the English Company at Surat, pursued local negotiations with the Viceroy at Goa. In January 1635 the Convention of Goa, signed by Methwold and Dom Miguel de Noronha, Conde de Linhares, permitted the English to enter and trade in Portugal's oriental ports and settlements.

Slow in agreeing to Methwold's terms, once the Convention was signed the Portuguese were quick in taking advantage of it. Within a few weeks an English ship, the *London*, was chartered by the viceregal government. She was reckoned sufficiently armed to meet opposition from Hollanders and pirates, and to bring back from Macao a valuable cargo that the Portuguese in their weakened state had no other means of obtaining, consisting of Japanese copper and some guns from Bocarro's foundry.

The English Company, with corresponding speed, agreed to charter. For them it was an opportunity to examine the China trade. A condition of the charter was therefore that English factors—commercial representatives of the English Company— should be carried to Macao and allowed to engage in business there.

Although the Viceroy acceded to this, among the Portuguese passengers were two other factors with secret orders not to allow the English to land at Macao. The Viceroy's position was delicate. The *London* was bearing the first news of the Convention. In view of Macao's uncompromisingly Portuguese spirit, it might be that the news would be ill-received. The Viceroy may not have been acting out of sheer duplicity. He had to play safe in the question of Macao's proud sentiments and quasi-independence.

Sailing from Surat in April 1635, the *London*, the first English ship to come to China, anchored at Macao on 23rd July. After an original refusal by the Macao authorities, the English were finally allowed ashore, factors and all, although a close watch was kept on them. Their presence being highly embarrassing, everything was done to have the copper and cannon loaded quickly, so that the vessel might depart with the first breath of autumn wind.

The Macanese, while appreciating the value of having a well-armed ship to carry their goods, saw at a glance that if the Chinese authorities noticed the newcomers there would be trouble, the difficulty being that in appearance the English resembled the Dutch, of whom the Chinese had formed a bad opinion. Needless to say, the Chinese did notice the English. Innocent of the intricacies of Macao, the English made as many contacts with Chinese as they could, promising to supply goods at lower rates than the Portuguese, if they should be allowed to return. And as the Macanese feared, the English were classed with the Dutch as barbarians of the new red species.

After the *London*'s departure, a fine was imposed on Macao for its negligence in allowing dangerous red barbarians into port. Fines on the city had become another Chinese method of punishing alleged misdemeanours. Whenever the Senate refused to pay and there was too much argument, pressure was applied. All Chinese—except Christians—were ordered to leave the city, which they invariably did at once. Having the nomadic temperament of squatters, and fearing to be involved in the least violence, the entire Chinese population, including those in the basements, left under no compulsion more deadly than the sight of an official notice. The barrier gate was closed behind them, and Macao's food supplies were cut off.

In earlier days, when the Portuguese had farms on Lappa, this treatment would have been ineffective, since the farms produced a good part of all the livestock and vegetables needed. But since 1600 the Macanese, with the easy self-assurance that everywhere robbed the Portuguese of the fruits of their enterprise, had allowed Cantonese labourers to cultivate parts of their farms, until gradually, with an act of kindness to a poor cultivator, or a debt paid here and there in exchange for a field, the cultivated land originally developed by Macao fell entirely into Cantonese hands.

The folly of allowing this to happen cannot be overstressed. With their slender defensive resources, the Macanese could not afford to be confined to their peninsula with nothing to feed them but the fields lying between the city and the barrier gate. As this area was required for grazing horses and cows, and was partly occupied, near the city wall and around Mong Ha temple, by Cantonese squatters' huts, it was only sparsely developed for agriculture, and then by Cantonese, not Portuguese. Once the Cantonese ran away, there was no one left who understood the slightest thing about farming.

As in Portugal under Manuel I and João III, so in Macao a century later: people could not be bothered with agriculture when it was so easy to buy food from outside. On the smallest pretext the Chinese could from henceforth starve Macao into doing exactly what it was told.

Christian persecution in Japan—end of Nagasaki as a trading port

Malacca—Macao—Nagasaki. It represented an age, one of the most remarkable trading epochs in history. But the loss of just one of these cities, and the commercial existence of the other two would be fatally threatened. Actually, all three were threatened and two were lost for the purposes of Portuguese trade, in the events that now befell, and which expunged the great Japan trade so completely that, within quite a few years, there was in Macao no trace that it had ever existed.

In 1615 Japan came under the sway of a new paramount feudal ruler, Tokugawa Ieyasu, who, confronting the difficulties of keeping his country's feudal lords under a single leadership, took the most rigid precautions against any faction or power that might threaten his security. For political reasons, and not for any particular doctrinal views he may have had, he resumed with conviction the persecution of Christianity, which had been dealt with spasmodically by his predecessors. Apart from the possibility that, through Christianity, the Spaniards in the Philippines might attempt to colonize Japan, there was the danger that rival feudal leaders in Japan, uniting themselves under the banner of Christianity, might offer resistance to Ieyasu's rule, a situation which would automatically invite the Spaniards in to assist them.

In 1616 the anti-Christian edict of Hideyoshi was re-enacted, and again in 1624. Although the principal foreign influence feared was that of Spain, the Portuguese influence in Nagasaki was not much less disliked. Missionaries were forbidden to enter the country. As some of them still managed to get in with the traders, a Japanese official agent was established at Macao, with orders to prevent missionaries from sailing to Japan, and to persuade as many as possible of Macao's Japanese community, which by this date included non-Christians as well as Christians, to return to their native land. The practice started of removing the rudders of foreign shipping entering Japanese ports, and not returning them till Japanese officials were satisfied that all orders had been complied with.

In the third Tokugawa shogun, Iemitsu (1623–51), foreign influence found its most determined and radical opponent. In 1636 the Portuguese and other foreigners were thrown out of

Nagasaki, the city that owed its greatness to them, and confined with the Dutch and others to a small artificial islet called Deshima, where alone trade with Europeans was permitted. Deshima was connected with the Nagasaki waterfront by a bridge, across which no European was allowed.

The next year, a feudal uprising took place in the Nagasaki peninsula, the inhabitants of which were largely Christian. As every intelligent Portuguese family realized, there could be only one outcome of this. As Iemitsu put his forces into the field to suppress the rebels, Portuguese morale sank into despair and panic. By every possible means, in junks and small boats, the Portuguese fled with what few possessions and money they could carry away.

Iemitsu began his suppression of the rebellion efficiently, and ended it savagely, in a massacre not only of the rebels, but of every Christian man, woman, and child he could find in the region. This, known as the Shimabara massacre, finally extinguished the open profession of Christianity in Japan. For Japan's and the Tokugawa family's safety, it effectively removed the danger of internal rebellion aided from without by Spain. It is nonetheless one of the blackest deeds in Japanese history, darkening the name of Iemitsu for ever. The Dutch, too, played a despicable part in the massacre. Anxious to ingratiate themselves with Iemitsu's government, they assisted in the reduction of Shimabara, bombarding from the sea this last stronghold of Japanese Christianity.

The horror of the massacre was brought home to Macao by the refugees who throughout 1638 continued to stream out of Japan by every means available. No exaggeration could have made the Christian persecution sound worse than it actually was, for Iemitsu stopped at no atrocity, however ghastly, in order to stamp out the alien cult for ever. The descriptions of the ways in which the Christians in Japan were forced to meet their deaths rank among the most horrifying and degraded reading-matter to be found anywhere.

For the Japan trade, there remained the islet of Deshima, where for the Portuguese knew that any moment the holocaust of Shimabara might be repeated. No Christian was allowed to leave the islet, the rudders of all ships were confiscated, and what little trade remained was under strict scrutiny. Deshima was in fact like a prison, particularly after the old freedom and ease of Nagasaki. The nervous strain of living unarmed, in constant fear of arrest, torture, or crucifixion, was more than most Portuguese could stand. Evacuation continued steadily, and by the end of 1639 only the Dutch, willing to discipline themselves to these conditions, were left.

Further restrictive edicts were issued by Iemitsu. No Japanese was allowed to leave the country; the construction of ocean-going ships was forbidden; no foreign ships could call at Japanese ports; and for fear their sojourn abroad had tainted them with Christianity, no Japanese overseas were allowed to return home. By a single stroke, the Japanese communities in Manila, Macao, Ayuthia, Malacca, and other cities of South-East Asia were exiled for ever, while Japan settled down to more than two centuries of isolation from the rest of the world.

End of Macao's trade with China—fall of Malacca—ruin of Portuguese Asia

The Japan trade was Macao's golden egg, but there still remained open a number of other lines of commerce, less spectacular but moderately lucrative—with Canton, Manila, various Indo-Chinese ports, and with Malacca and Goa. In an astonishingly rapid series of misfortunes, all of this was ripped away as well.

1637 saw the first English trading voyage to China, four ships under the command of Captain John Weddell, with the diarist Peter Mundy as factor. In the course of this visit, the

English ships penetrated far up the Pearl River without Chinese permission, blew up a fort, burnt one village and raided several others, and murdered a number of Chinese. They finally departed in all humility, having been eased out jointly by the Chinese and the Portuguese; but Weddell's voyage had established the thenceforth unchanging Chinese view that, of all barbarian intruders, the English were the most violent and dangerous.

The Chinese authorities demanded an immense sum from Macao as a fine for Weddell's intrusion. When the Senate remonstrated, Canton replied by making further-reaching demands, saying that the first English ship to call at Macao, the *London*, had been under-assessed for tonnage dues. So began a wrangle lasting several years, in an atmosphere of threats, sudden alarms, strictures, and severe warnings, the stock in trade of the Chinese civil service.

In 1640 the dispute reached deadlock. The Macanese were no longer able to provide China with the Japanese silver she desired in exchange for her silk and porcelain. Nor could they provide spices, control of the spice trade having passed from Portuguese to Dutch hands. China was not interested in any of Europe's bulk exports, and Indian cotton was a poor substitute for silver. Macao being of little further use, the Chinese authorities made the English irruption an excuse for forbidding future Portuguese attendance at the trade fairs. The port of Canton was closed to them.

The two greatest lines, with China and Japan, were thus broken. Those with Manila and Malacca remained. An attempt to re-open the route to Japan failed, the Portuguese envoys sent to negotiate at Nagasaki being beheaded.

In the same year a revolution took place in Lisbon. The Duke of Bragança, a descendant of the old royal house, was proclaimed King João IV of Portugal. The following year, 1641, when the news reached the Far East, the Portuguese went wild with joy. In Manila they caused disturbances, and in Macao they celebrated the occasion by a characteristic reaction of exuberant folly: they expelled the entire Spanish community, thereby themselves cutting one of their remaining trade links.

Within a few weeks, the Dutch attacked and seized Malacca, and the cobweb of restriction sewn around Macao was complete. The Governor of the Philippines made an attempt to secure Macao under Spanish control, but popular feeling was so hostile to Spain that Macao's Captain-General, Sebastião Lobo da Silveira, who as a Spanish appointee felt a certain loyalty to the Castilian Crown, was obliged to concede to the people's wish and formally side Macao with the revolution.

This was not enough for Macao, however. There was an element of duplicity in Lobo da Silveira's handling of the situation. A body of armed citizens broke into his house, found him hiding under the stairs, and in a joint assassination cut him to death with sword and dagger. So much for Spain. So much for any of hesitant loyalty to the house of Bragança.

Cut off from Japan, China, the Philippines, and even from Goa, Macao clung bravely and unyieldingly to her Portuguese identity amid the wreckage of her people's extraordinary achievements. Of the splendid lands and seas Portugal had opened to European enterprise, hardly anything in Asia remained to her. For the seas, with their pirates and rivals, her ships and armament were too weak; on land, all that she still precariously held was a handful of insignificant ports in India and Ceylon, two small settlements in the Indies—a segment of the island of Timor, and the islet of Solor—and Macao.

Yet a Portuguese is never too poor to make a brave gesture, and in 1642 the pitiable city sent a gift of guns and money—as much as could be scraped together—to the new king, with a pledge of loyalty to him.

João IV was an unusual person to be the figurehead of a revolution: a quiet, plain-spoken man, interested in music. It is said that when he learnt where Macao was, and in what plight, he remarked wonderingly at its people's faith in him; and his words—'*Não ha outra mais leal*'—with the implied sadness in them of a monarch who could do nothing to help, were shortly before his death proudly included in the city's motto, borne ever since, commemorating Macao's faith and tenacity in the worst moments of her history: 'City of the Name of God, None Other More Loyal'.

Brave gestures—irresistible to the Portuguese—misplaced generosity, lack of economic shrewdness, an absurdly legalistic and restrictive conception of authority in relation to commerce: these, coupled with the ill-effects of union with Spain, caused Portuguese Asia to wither before it was full-grown.

By 1640 the Portuguese language was the international medium of commerce along the entire vast littoral of Africa and Asia; but throughout the territories discovered by the Portuguese other Europeans were installed. There were still thousands of Portuguese in Asia, but they had drifted off into the bodyguards of Hindu maharajas and Buddhist kings, to fight in Burmese and Talaing wars, to man the ships of Asian merchants and pirates, or engage in trade of their own in a multitude of small ports—Martaban, Mergui, Acheh, Champa, and others that exist no more. They had succeeded the Malays in the reputation of being the most reliable mercenaries in the East.

There is something awe-inspiring about Portugal's colossal achievement, and the suddenness and completeness of the disaster that followed it. One is not conscious of it in Macao, where the atmosphere is one of cultural continuity. It is in Lisbon that it can be understood, in the great abbey church of the Jerónimos at Belém, built by Dom Manuel as a monument of thanksgiving to God, celebrating the triumph of his navigators over the most distant seas.

Technically the greatest achievement of the Jerónimos, and of the manueline style itself, is the transept, the work of João de Castilho, dating from about 1522. The widest gothic transept in Europe, the almost incredible span achieved by the arches is the superlative example of the manueline architects' ability to encompass space without massive ground support. The pillars of the main arch of the transept are only slightly thicker than the other four slender pillars of the nave, the lightness of the design creating a wonderful sensation of spaciousness.

In the nave, in two unspectacular neo-manueline tombs, are commemorated the two men whose names above all others will for ever be linked with the glories of Dom Manuel's reign—Vasco da Gama, who gave the reign its glory, and Portugal's greatest poet, Luis Vaz de Camões, who, when the glory had passed away, spelled it out in his incomparable verse. There is one striking similarity between the two men, rendering it more than fitting that they should be commemorated side by side. Each achieved what he did in a life of gruelling frustration and disappointment.

Once the tumult of his welcome home had subsided, Vasco da Gama found himself in the unenviable position of being an inconveniently portentous figure. The most celebrated navigator of the age, and one of its most skilled diplomats, he was larger than life itself, with the result that his country, having praised him, deemed it wiser to ignore him. For nearly twenty years after his two momentous voyages to India he lived in comparative obscurity, guardedly—almost exaggeratedly—wearing black unadorned by the slightest ornament. Finally, in 1524, when Goa, instead of blazoning forth as the shining example of Christian virtue once hoped for, had on the contrary sunk into the lowest depths of oriental corruption, Vasco da

Gama, an ageing patriarch with his long white beard, was appointed Viceroy of India, in the hope that he would set the Portuguese empire morally on its feet again. Within four months of his arrival in Goa he was dead. They had sent for him again at last, but too late.

As for Camões, that he should figure in this sepulchre of kings is, when one considers the endless trouble he had with the authorities of his time, a superb irony, rendered bitter by the way his country let him die. He died in such complete poverty that no one knows what became of his body. The tomb is empty.

There beneath the manueline vault of the Jerónimos, enclosed in a gothic masterpiece, lies in its strange completeness the tale of Portugal's greatest age. Standing within the unique dimensions of João de Castilho's transept, one can look about at each one of them where they lie: Manuel I, the Fortunate, lord of the commerce of Africa and Asia; João III, who laid the foundations of another empire in Brazil; Sebastião, who threw away the achievements of two centuries on the sands of Alcâcer-Quebir (his tomb is empty); and his doddering great-uncle, Cardinal Henrique, whose obstinate refusal to name a Portuguese heir, even on his deathbed, ushered in the sixty years of the Union of the Crowns.

Few monuments erected to celebrate a triumph have chronicled so complete a disaster; few disasters have been memorialized beside such triumph in so complete a work of art.

6

Outpost of All Europe

The British in Macao

The years following the ending of the Japan trade were the darkest Macao has ever lived through, and they lasted a long time, during which the city became dreadfully impoverished and was in danger of extinction.

They were also years which marked an equally dreadful deterioration in morale. Victims of mob murders included a governor and a head of the Senate. The famous Dominican friar Domingo Navarrete, who was there in 1670, wrote, 'It would take up much time and paper to write but a small Epitome of the Broils, Uproars, Quarrels and Extravagancies there have been at Macao.' Some years earlier, in 1649, the factor of an English voyage referred to 'Maccaw itselfe soe distracted amongst themselves that they are dailie spilling one anothers blood'.

With it came the irrational: endless insistence on Portuguese superiority in all fields, blame of Spain for every iota in Portugal's catalogue of disaster, and incontrovertible assertion of Portugal's sovereignty over Macao, a situation which was rather belied when the Governor of Kwangtung closed the barrier gate and only opened it twice a month, when the better-off purchased a fortnight's provisions while the rest starved.

Sixty years passed before, with the beginning of regular British trade with China, from the year 1700 onward, there was a very slight improvement in Macao internal conditions.

During the eighteenth century, the volume of European trade with China, all of it through Canton, rose steadily. French, Dutch, Danes, Swedes, and Spaniards all participated, with

Britain's trade double the volume of all the rest put together. Foreigners being required by the Chinese authorities to leave Canton at the end of each trading season, nearly all the principal traders in this cosmopolitan community needed residence rights in Macao, enabling them to pass the summer there, before going up to Canton for the next season.

Here the foreigners found themselves in a quagmire of Portuguese restrictions, most of them belonging to Portugal's golden age, now completely outdated. As seen earlier, there was considerable latitude during that age for such foreigners as spoke Portuguese, used a Portuguese name, and were or pretended to be Catholic. In the eighteenth century no one was prepared to put up with so esoteric an entry system, which was in any case by this time totally unrealistic.

Adding to the difficulties, the majority of the foreigners were Protestants, and none of them were allowed by the Chinese authorities to bring women with them, with an inevitable impact on Macao's night-life. The ecclesiastical authorities were thus the most opposed to foreign residence, and making things still more difficult, from 1691 onward Macao had had a Bishop.

Just as the first Captain-General was seen as an encroachment on the city's quasi-independence, so in another sphere was the Bishop. Between them, the Governor and the Bishop surcharged the atmosphere with authority, preventing the unfortunate population from enjoying the benefits that a resident foreign community would undoubtedly bring them. Importance was attached to the corrupting influence of the cosmopolitan crowd of bachelors—or at any rate men whose wives were never likely to come to China—who had succeeded in wangling their way in during the summer as lodgers. Minor laws were made to protect the Macanese from their poisonous ways. In 1744, local-born men were forbidden to wear wigs and ruffles, symbols of loose-living English beaux; and two years later, through church influence, Lisbon issued a decree making foreign residence at Macao illegal, even for lodgers. The decree was not completely effective; some lodgers remained. Staying without the law, however, with no redress to authority in the event of trouble, their position was unpleasantly insecure. At last, but not until 1757, the Senate managed to convince both the Governor and the faraway Viceroy at Goa of the wisdom of their demands, the Bishop was overridden, and the more vexatious restrictions against foreigners were withdrawn.

From that moment, and rapidly, Macao entered upon another remarkable period. It became in effect the outpost of all Europe in China—indeed, the centre and fulcrum of foreign relations with China—a position it held for more than eighty years, until 1841, when with the foundation of Hongkong, and the opening of Shanghai and the other Treaty Ports to foreign residence, a new era began.

Although the changes of 1757 brought benefits to Macao, her shipyards were once again active, and her trade improved, notably with India, it cannot be said that the presence of (above all) the British made things socially easy for the Portuguese. It was a cuckoo-in-the-nest situation, and this accentuated when, in the first decade of the nineteenth century, Englishwomen ignored Chinese regulations by taking residence in Macao with their husbands and children, living a life of their own, an aloof, grander, and much wealthier life than that of the local people. In fact, for much of the period the British behaved virtually as if the Portuguese did not exist, and the Americans and others were not much better.

Dominating the British community throughout most of this period were the commercial officers of the Honourable East India Company Trading to China. Their imposing premises were in the best position on the Praia Grande—four large residential buildings joined together internally, mounting the hill they culminated in another set of entrance on the Ridge. The East India Company was the largest commercial organization on earth, and no one was left in any doubt about it. Everything concerned with it was on the grand scale.

Its chief, known as the President of the Select Committee, had as his official residence the finest property in the place—today the Camões Museum—with a garden so extensive that it included all the present-day public places around it, including the Rocks of Camões. These had not yet been developed into a memorial, but the tradition about them was well-known, as was the work of Camões himself to the highly educated men who formed the senior staff of the Company. The President's distinguished visitors were invariably shown the rocks.

It was this acquisition, more than anything else, that symbolized and summed up the social situation. Owning the Rock of Camões, after all, was rather like having someone else's national monument in one's back garden.

And in Portugal

Dislike and mistrust of the British were deepened in Macao by the ever-increasing influence reported from Portugal. As with the pepper from Asia, so with the gold from Brazil: the wealth unexpectedly placed in Portuguese hands slipped through the fingers in a short time, bringing little or no benefit to country and people as a whole. While Dom João V (1706–50) lavished his wealth on buildings of sensational opulence, including the magnificent university library at Coimbra, and on the chilling solemnity of his palace-cum-basilica at Mafra, government become steadily more priest-ridden, and sank into profound administrative lethargy. Well might the king, the wealthiest monarch in Europe, with unprecedented pomp wash the feet of the poor, and send a glittering embassy to China scattering largesse in the streets of Peking, at home his soldiers were reduced to begging for food at the doors of convents, while entire districts of fertile land lay uncultivated, the roads being impassable due to long neglect. Strange to relate, João V at his death was greatly mourned; as one writer caustically put it, 'The poor rather like having their feet washed in grand state.'

During the reign of José I (1750–77) the country came under the dictatorship of the king's favourite and chief minister, the Marquês de Pombal, a man from whom, whatever his attainments, one ends by turning one's face away in revulsion at his vindictive cruelty and the horror of his persecutions. Pombal had nonetheless a zealous desire to rid Portugal of old abuses. If a vote for or against him had been taken in Macao, the majority would have been for him. Macao saw him as a strong man, modernizing Portugal, curbing the mercantile power of the British (the state within the State, just as it was in Macao), reorganizing the Brazilian goldmines, suppressing slavery and smuggling. They did not see him amassing a vast private fortune, or placing his relatives and creatures in key posts. Nor did they see the ineffectualness of his rule, during which Portugal's volume of trade dropped by nearly two-thirds in twenty years. While splendid edicts were sent out, such as one to Macao abolishing slavery, the army had no pay for years, and the prisons were filled with thousands of untried members of the nobility, and with Jesuit fathers, two-thirds of whom succumbed before the doors were at last opened in what the Spanish ambassador described as a resurrection of the dead.

The moment King José breathed his last, Pombal was dismissed. The country was financially and administratively in stagnation, from which only a cabinet of supermen could have extricated it. The new government was faced with two decades of debts, unpaid employees, and unanswered ministerial letters, and a capital still largely in ruins as a result of the disastrous earthquake of 1755, the most terrible earthquake in European history.

The mild, benign rule of Dom José's daughter, Maria I, proved to be what was needed. Very slowly the country got into its stride again, only to be menaced by war with Spain, the ally of revolutionary France. The Queen, a sympathetic and tragic figure, found herself obliged to annul, undo, or reverse one after another of Pombal's edicts and decisions, all of them sanctioned by her father. The inherent betrayal in this finally overwhelmed her, and she became insane. Holding open court in the exquisite intimacy of the palace of Queluz, just outside Lisbon, accessible to everyone high and low, had she reigned in the twentieth century she would have been one of the most popular of all monarchs. But reigning after Pombal was no easy matter for a person as sensitive as she. From 1792 her son took over as Prince Regent.

During this reign of national revival, after the unprecedented reign of terror that preceded it, individual Britons, in commerce and even in the Portuguese Army, rose to positions of extraordinary prominence. A Scot, John Forbes Skellater, commanded a large section of the Army, and British professional troops were stationed in the country to reinforce the wretchedly neglected Portuguese soldiery. From Macao it looked as if Portugal was falling completely beneath British domination.

In Macao itself, it was a variant of the same condition. There the British did not infiltrate the governmental machine. They simply ignored it, and did exactly as they pleased. The meanest Briton considered himself superior to the loftiest Portuguese, and few in authority dared lay a finger on any of them, least of all on those in the service of the formidable East India Company. All things considered, it is surprising the British behaved themselves as well as they did; individuals were seldom a cause of serious trouble.

Miguel de Arriaga and Thomas Beale

The threat from Spain materialized in October 1807, when the forces of Napoleonic France, under Marshal Junot, invaded Portugal in what was, to start with, virtually a walk-over. The Prince Regent and his family fled to Brazil, and the Court re-assembled in Rio de Janeiro.

It was fear that Spain, from Manila, might try to take over Macao, which in 1808 led to the most extraordinary incident of the period, when the British forcibly occupied Macao with troops of their own, sent from India. Chinese official reaction to this was explosive, to put it mildly. The Governor was told that unless he rid Chinese soil of British troops, a Chinese army would be sent to do so for him. Realizing full well that this last must at all costs be prevented, since for the Portuguese it would be the end, some tense, three-sided negotiations followed, the British forces were withdrawn, and the Chinese authorities were pacified.

Central to the solution of this difficult affair was Macao's judge, Miguel de Arriaga. One of the most intriguing figures of the time, he was one of those able, devious, and cunning men, of whom Macao has experienced a number, whose commercial and personal ties with the Chinese have been so extensive that in emergencies they have been capable of serving political ends.

For the judge, contrary to the rules of his calling, was in commerce. His nefarious dealings might well have escaped the attention of history, had it not been for his connexion with Thomas Beale, who was for many years the city's wealthiest and most experienced opium dealer.

Beale lived in Macao for more than fifty years, and was the best-known of all the foreigners of his time. Stately in bearing, rather formal, with old-fashioned manners, he occupied one of finest of the older Portuguese houses, enclosed within high walls, as the best properties were in those days, on a narrow street known to foreigners as Beale's Lane. The privilege of viewing his garden, which was one of the sights of the city, was something no visitor wished to miss; and he kept a remarkable aviary of rare birds, collected by his agents from all over East Asia.

Beale's was general agency business, of course, but by far the most profitable commodity he handled, and the most dangerous, was opium—dangerous because it was a prohibited import, and because, dependent on the degree of Chinese vigilance, it was subject to sudden drastic price fluctuations.

Traffic through Macao, though, was relatively easy. The Chinese customs were geared to deal with the Canton trade, which was far more important than that of Macao, and Beale, like many others, had been doing well in Macao for years. He looked confidently ahead to retirement with a fortune.

But to a speculator a new opportunity never comes too late, and Beale had invested in something promising truly spectacular returns. Counting on the great influence of Miguel de Arriaga and his aristocrat son-in-law, the Baron São João de Porto Alegre—Beale had gone into partnership of an informal kind with the Judge, on a basis of shared profit and loss. The speculation was in opium, and in trade with Brazil, where the two Portuguese intended to pull strings. It seems that in the preparatory stages of the venture, most of the money used was Beale's. Some of it went on bribes to officials in Rio, some on the worthless son-in-law's expenses, and a great deal was probably spent by Arriaga himself on the sumptuous living for which he was famous. Perhaps they really had expectations of pulling off an enormous deal; perhaps the entire affair was a fraud. No one will ever know. In fact, the matter would never have come to light had it not coincided with a sudden change in the opium situation.

In 1815 the Governor of Kwangtung unexpectedly arrested several Chinese opium dealers, and ordered searches of all ships entering Macao and Whampoa, the port of Canton. The sudden Chinese action knocked the bottom out of the market.

Beale was caught with several hundred chests of opium, for which, as was customary, he had already drawn bills on the East India Company, payable in Calcutta. The opium was his security for these, cash to be paid over after a month or so, when the drug was sold. His chests being now unsaleable, he found himself owing the East India Company nearly half a million dollars.

The situation had a graver aspect than would seem. Quite apart from the size of the debt, the Select Committee of the East India Company would be obliged to admit to their superiors, the Council in Calcutta, that it was their practice to issue bills for opium instead of for cash, treating the drug itself as if it were money. This practice had been going on for years, but no one in Calcutta or London had ever been told about it. The fat was now in the fire, and Beale, the cause of it, could expect no mercy.

His only hope was Arriaga. If he could withdraw some of the money he had put into their joint speculation, he might yet be saved. Beale, who was in Canton at the time, hastily came down to Macao.

The honourable Judge, however, in spite of the magnificence of his home and table, was unused to demands for ready cash. What took place at Beale's interview with him is not known, but Arriaga's line of argument is clear. Beale's money was an investment, not a loan.

Arriaga was vain, able, and unscrupulous. By dealing with Chinese, Portuguese, Macanese and foreign resident, playing one off against another, he had created for himself a position of almost unchallengeable power. As a judge, he was not allowed to trade. He was nonetheless up to his neck in opium, in debt to an unfathomable extent, and, as his relations with Beale suggest, open to classification as little better than a confidence trickster. Yet, as already seen, when there was serious trouble over the British military occupation of Macao, it was Arriaga who alone was considered capable of handling the situation, who used his unique influence with the Chinese, and appeared as the saviour of the city. He was, too.

The unfortunate Beale did receive some help from his august partner, though not much in comparison with his investment. The fact of the matter was that, having been so foolhardy as to engage in business in Rio, which was the exclusive right of Portuguese citizens, in partnership with a judge who was not allowed to trade at all, he had only himself to thank if things went wrong.

By a great effort Beale paid the East India Company about half the sum he owed them—he had drawn bills in advance of opium sales worth $800,000—and in Macao a small sum was scraped together to pay off some more. As for the rest, if Porto Alegre had frittered a great deal of it away in Rio, it was regrettable. Arriaga, suave and calculating, fingering the jewelled decoration on his breast, was not prepared to ruin his own reputation to save Beale's.

Thomas Beale was declared bankrupt, with the East India Company as principal creditor. To avoid any ignominious scenes, he slipped away from his beautiful home, to take refuge somewhere in secret; and he was never found—itself an achievement in so small a place as Macao.

The proceedings to investigate his debts went on for several years, and had to be handled with discretion. No Macao lawyer could be found even to advise on so dangerous a case, involving the puissant judge. When confronted with the facts as known to the Company, Arriaga smoothly denied that he owed Beale anything. From the investigation his debt appeared to be well over one and a half million dollars, but in view of Arriaga's power, if the Company was ever to receive justice, it could only be by appeal to Rio de Janeiro, and there of course Arriaga's writ would still run, thanks to the aristocrat son-in-law.

After the initial excitement subsided, Beale came back quietly to his house, where he managed to keep going modestly for many years afterwards, a ruined man, dodging creditors and keeping up a dignified appearance on borrowed money and small agency business. Like the opium trade that had broken him, he was tolerated, being left to live with his regrets. And as his creditors, the Company, would pounce on him the moment he made enough money to return to England, he was doomed to die on the China coast.

Revolution in Macao

The end of the Napoleonic War was in Portugal a time of disillusion. The Congress of Vienna awarded a miserable sum in reparations from the French for all the devastation inflicted by them during the war. British power in Portugal was stronger than ever. A Briton, Lord Beresford, was actually Commander-in-Chief of the Portuguese Army, with powers that, in the absence of any restraining authority, amounted to dictatorship. The Court remained in Rio de Janeiro.

But the Napoleonic invasion of Portugal, if it achieved nothing else, brought with it some of the sparks that kindled the French Revolution. From 1817 to 1820 popular dissatisfaction found voice in a series of disorders and liberal uprisings, aimed at the removal of Beresford and the return to Portugal of the former Prince Regent, now King João VI.

These events echoed in Macao in a way peculiar to the city's special and unusual traditions. The Portuguese liberal movement was applauded by a majority of Macanese, to whom liberalism meant the restoration of the old prestige of the Senate, the abolition of the Governor's veto over its administrative decisions, and the termination of the corrupt rule of aristocratic officials appointed by Rio and Goa. Foremost among these, the most powerful and unpopular, was Judge Arriaga, whose known anti-liberal views and autocratic conduct made him the chief enemy of those disgruntled factions conveniently styled liberal.

In 1821 a liberal revolution broke out in Brazil, persuading João VI at last to return to Portugal. Before he arrived, however, a similar revolution had taken place there as well. The King reached Lisbon to find himself a constitutional monarch.

In Macao, Governor Castro Cabral called a meeting at which everyone swore allegiance to the new constitution of Portugal. Beneath the surface, however, the higher officials and aristocrats in Goa and Macao disliked the liberal movement, and were doubtful of adhering to it, considering that as soon as he had sufficient power in Portugal, the King would seek to overthrow it. In Macao there was the additional consideration that a change of government of this kind would certainly be misunderstood by the Chinese authorities, to whom any departure from unquestioning obedience to a king would seem a dangerous development.

Royal permission for the constitution to be introduced in Macao had not been received before the quasi-liberals took matters into their own hands. At a meeting of the Senate in August 1822, a document was presented accusing Arriaga of conspiring with the Chinese to prevent the adoption of the constitution. Two days later, the liberals ordered a re-election of the Senate, the restoration of its former powers, and the dismissal of Arriaga from all his offices. Castro Cabral retained his position as Governor, though divested of all administrative responsibility.

These changes were scarcely accomplished when there burst upon the city a portent of a new age, a weekly newspaper. In the days of the old Jesuit ascendancy, Macao was an important printing centre, producing many well-printed books, principally concerned with the propagation of Christianity in Far Eastern countries. By the early seventeenth century these activities had diminished in importance, and in the middle of the eighteenth century an order was made forbidding printing in Portuguese colonies. Under the influence of the liberal movement in Portugal, this ban was lifted in 1820. A printing press was promptly ordered by Macao from Lisbon. It arrived just in time to participate in the revolution.

The newspaper—it was the first printed newspaper in the Far East—was called *Abelha da China*—Bee of China—and was edited by the Principal of the Dominicans who, of all people, was a determined liberal. The new rule allowing printing in colonies was not quite so liberal as it looked at first sight. All material printed had to be censored before publication. Nevertheless, in the hands of a clever editor there was reasonable breadth of opportunity, as *Abelha da China* proceeded to demonstrate.

Throughout the autumn the re-elected Senate carried on shakily. Their opponents, however, were as inexperienced as themselves in the art of Latin politics, and early in 1823 a revolt, badly organized by the opposition, to install a military régime in place of the Senate, was put down after a mere skirmish in the streets. After this, Governor Castro Cabral, held to be implicated in the military revolt, was deposed and imprisoned in Monte fort. Arriaga too was arrested.

The downfall of the corrupt judge could hardly have been more complete. The moment his dismissal from office was announced, many to whom he owed money had pressed in upon him for payment, while others whom he had wronged joined in vilifying him. Unable to pay even a small percentage of the debts accumulated over years of careless extravagance, his health broke down, and pending deportation he was allowed to reside at his house.

It was arranged for him and Castro Cabral to leave in the same ship, to be tried in Goa for their offences against the new constitution. But Arriaga, the old fox, was not going to risk his life among his own countrymen when there were others among whom he could enjoy perfect safety. During the embarkation in Macao roads, he managed to slip aboard a fastboat, which made off immediately for Canton, outdistancing its pursuers.

The Viceroy of Portuguese India meanwhile sent a frigate, the *Salamandra*, in support of the deposed Governor. The Senate refused to admit the vessel, supply her, or allow her troops to land. When the commander of *Salamandra* showed signs of effecting a landing by force, the forts of Macao were manned by citizens and guns were loaded. The commander, thereupon preparing to bombard, issued a warning to all Chinese to leave the city for forty-eight hours.

At this moment of extreme tension, a group of Chinese officials arrived from Canton to mediate—such was the extent of Arriaga's influence. Though their visit achieved nothing positive, it delayed a settlement; and in the anti-climax it created, the ardour of the constitutionalists cooled. Their leaders were still recommending reforms and new procedures; but when their supporters reflected that the really important things for Macao were after all opium and rents from foreigners, it was difficult to sustain interest in politics.

One could look round at the British, for example. There they were, throughout the whole affair, taking no notice whatever. A baffling people. Even under threat of bombardment, they carried on as usual.

In truth, few of the British knew what was happening. Incidents such as the Governor's imprisonment provided the ladies with plenty to talk about, but no one pretended to understand Portuguese politics. Moreover, extraordinary as it might seem in a Portuguese city, to the British community whoever won it made no difference. The revolution was like a comic opera in which they, as spectators, had by accident been seated in the middle of the stage, surrounded by the singers.

The commander of *Salamandra* now did some careful timing. When he calculated that enthusiasm had exhausted itself, he landed his troops without opposition, arrested the revolutionary leaders, kept the peace while autocracy was reinstated by a provisional government under the Bishop, witnessed a *volte-face* popular outcry for the return of Arriaga (who did a quick change from villain to hero), and sailed away to Goa with the ringleaders of reform under arrest.

The foreign community sighed, thinking it was the final curtain. There was still another act to come, however. Some months later, news arrived from Portugal of Prince Miguel's public championship of his father's rights as an absolute monarch. Macao went wild with joy. For three nights there were illuminations, processions, and banquets.

The foreign spectators could only presume they had lost the thread of the story. Nothing seemed to make sense any more. But Macanese went to bed happy. If the spectators had not understood it, the singers had. Not for them the French Revolution. The Bishop would never stand for it.

Return to autocracy

Opium was mentioned just now as being important to Macao. This was the one and only time when it was.

Ever since the annual auctions of Bengal opium were inaugurated in India, the Portuguese had dealt in the drug through Calcutta, where there was a large and fairly influential Portuguese community. Lacking the resources to bid on a large scale, however, their trade in it was modest; Indian cotton was a far more important item in their cargoes. Large-scale opium commerce was British and American.

Americans were first seen on the Praia Grande in 1784. As was to become typical of them, the *Empress of China*, in which they arrived, was one of the fastest sailing ships in the world. It was in Macao, too, that the Chinese, on first sight of the Stars and Stripes, gave the flag its Chinese name, the 'Flowery Banner', which has endured ever since.

The Americans quickly rose to a place second only to the British in the China trade. By the time of the Napoleonic Wars, almost all China coast trade was either British or American. The British traded in Bengal opium from Calcutta, the Americans in Turkish opium from Smyrna.

There was a third important source of opium. This was Malwa, in western India, for which the most convenient port was Bombay. Malwa was not yet under British rule, and its opium was posing such a commercial threat to Bengal (British) opium that in 1813 the East India Company placed restrictions on the export of Malwa opium through Bombay. This automatically threw the trade into an almost equally convenient port, Damão, and into the hands of the Portuguese.

Needless to say, this had an electrifying effect on Macao. The Macanese were going to enter the big stakes; they would beat the British at their own game.

For a few months it looked as though they might. But as on so many former occasions, they wrecked their own chances by the legalisms in which the trade was enmeshed. From Damão, opium—indeed, any commodity—had to be conveyed in ships of Portuguese register, bound for a Portuguese destination. At

Macao, it had to pass through the Portuguese customs, which, faced with such a windfall, charged excessively high dues, and it could then be handled only by Portuguese agents, rendering the entire business even less economical.

Private British traders, by this time omnipresent throughout the East, chartered vessels of Portuguese register, and brought the opium from Damão to the island of Lintin, in the Pearl River, where it was off-loaded and stored in mastless hulks, against the time of safe delivery to Canton. When they reached Macao, they had no opium aboard. In due course they made matters still easier for themselves by bribing officials in Goa to issue passes exempting British ships from the Portuguese regulations. Ninety per cent of the Malwa windfall never went near Macao.

The reaction of the Macanese needs no description. So high had been their hopes, they had seen Malwa opium in terms of a revival of Macao's ancient glories. Seldom was there such hostility toward the British as when these hopes were dashed.

To cap it, the year 1821 witnessed another 'great threatening' by the Governor of Kwangtung on the issue of opium. This time, Chinese vigilance extended to Macao, and the degree of it was so intense that it was unsafe to move even small quantities of the drug from one building to another. All opium had to be packaged to look like something else. When this was discovered, house searches were threatened, and some evidently took place. Possession of the drug became so dangerous that people were reduced to burying opium in their gardens, hastily planting above the buried chests the fastest-growing flowers, one would assume. Britons and Americans, as a result of the scare of 1821, moved every ounce of opium out of Macao, and swore never to use the place again for its storage.

This was the economic background against which the constitutional revolution just described took place.

One of the first casualties in the return to autocracy was *Abelha da China*, which paid the price of having turned from a bee into a wasp during the revolution. Arriaga suppressed it, replacing it by the more sedate *Gazeta de Macau*.

But Macao without opium was a city in which Arriaga was a stranger. Although as judge he was reinstated, the epoch in which he prospered had already passed away, and in what was left of Macao after it, Arriaga had no place. He died in 1824, less than a year after his reinstatement, and was followed within a few months by his son-in-law, 'the Baron'. Most daring of all Macao's opium magnates, and the most spendthrift of his gains, São João de Porto Alegre was for years the agent of some of the leading British firms. Not even he could survive the strangulation of Macao by the Malwa traders. Struggling to the last to keep in business, he died in the true heart of the opium trade, Calcutta.

Both he and Arriaga left incalculable debts. For another five years, until 1830, the inexorable East India Company pursued its rights in the Beale affair, until at last they were written off as losses. As for old Beale himself, with Arriaga and Baron dead, and ten years behind him to soften the outlines of the scandal, he felt more free to live a normal life again. Once more he opened his house and beautiful garden to visiting friends.

It was a façade, however. He was slowly running himself into a new chain of debts. Eventually he withdrew from his house, and went to live with his compradore, one of the many Chinese creditors who, out of respect for his age, never pressed him for payment. In 1841, apparently reduced to literally his last, he committed suicide on the lonely sands of Cacilhas Bay.

First steps at tourist attraction

Of the many old restrictions placed on foreigners in Macao, one on which the ecclesiastical authorities refused to relent concerned burial. None but a Catholic might be buried in what was deemed to be Catholic soil, and this was taken to mean the whole of Macao within the walls.

The burial of a Protestant thus had to take place in the area between the walls and the barrier gate. It had to be conducted as secretly as possible, and in as remote a place as possible, since if a Chinese saw a foreign burial in progress, he would quickly band together with others, and offer resistance to it. Interments sometimes took place under armed guard, and were commonly an occasion of yelled obscenities and fisticuffs. Once a body had been laid to rest amid one of these affrays, and the burial party returned to the city, it was wiser not to inquire the subsequent fate of the grave.

Chinese buried their dead in this area. As the years passed, there came to be thousands of Chinese tombs here. But for a foreigner to be laid to rest in Chinese soil was a desecration in the eye of heaven, a different heaven from the one within the walls, but equally insistent on the sacredness of its soil. A Protestant burial being a peculiarly horrible occasion, the Catholic restriction was one that aroused in foreigners a particular contempt.

In June 1821, Mary, wife of Robert Morrison, the first Protestant missionary in China—he was the East India Company's Chinese interpreter—died while on the point of giving birth to a child.

Morrison, who resided in Macao from 1807 until his death in 1834, was one of the most narrow-minded, humourless men ever to earn respect and fame for good works—his principal achievement was his translation of the Bible into Chinese—but the prospect that now lay before him constitutes one of the moments in his life when he commands absolute sympathy. None knew better than he the anguish of a Protestant funeral, and he was filled with foreboding at the thought of accompanying his wife's remains past insulting, jeering Cantonese crowds.

With the intention of burying the body near the hilltop tomb of his firstborn son, he went out north of the city with some labourers to dig the grave. There he was resisted by Cantonese squatters, who menacingly refused to allow him near the place. Pointing out to them that his child was already buried there, he begged them to allow him at least to re-open the child's grave and bury mother and son together, but the men still sullenly refused. In spite of having no rights themselves to the land, they could at will bring the Chinshan magistrate's flunkeys thundering into the city, and Morrison realized it was useless to argue with them. In the greatest misery he retraced his steps.

The alternative was to bury under the city walls. Owing to the large number of squatter huts clustered there, with the probability of the grave being spoiled or desecrated, he disliked having to do this; but as he later explained in a letter to his parents-in-law, he 'was obliged to resolve on doing so, as the Papists refuse their burying ground to Protestants.

'The want of a Protestant burying ground,' the letter continues, 'has long been felt in Macao, and the present case brought it strongly before the Committee of the English Factory, who immediately resolved to vote a sum sufficient to purchase a piece of ground, worth between three and four thousand dollars; and personally exerted themselves to remove the legal impediments and local difficulties; in which they finally succeeded. This enabled me to lay the remains of my beloved wife in a place appropriated to the sepulture of Protestant Christians, denied a place of interment by the Romanists.'

The East India Company's cemetery in Macao is in its small way one of the loveliest places in the Far East. Nothing of it can be seen from without. One rings a bell to be admitted.

Within is an enclosed garden, with flowering trees of great age planted on a falling, tiered slope. As the high wall and closing gates alienate the Chinese clatter of the street, so does the quiet atmosphere of an English cathedral city move envelopingly forward. It is like the garden of a presbytery that was once a graveyard. Old and no longer tended, the gravestones have lost their bleak quality of chronicling sorrow. They have become as mellow as old walls, as friendly as books, until all is garden, with no associations more mournful than those evoked by old houses.

The site, just within the city wall, was part of the extensive gardens surrounding the mansion of the President of the Select Committee, the property as a whole being known to the British as the Casa Garden. The owner of the Casa Garden was Manuel Pereira, a wealthy merchant and financier, and a Portuguese privy councillor, the only person in Macao's history to receive this distinction. Pereira was on friendly terms with the British, and it was through him that application was made to the Governor for permission for Pereira to sell a piece of the Casa Garden land to the Company.

The Governor, Castro Cabral, despite the Portuguese law preventing foreign ownership of land, sanctioned the transaction on his personal responsibility, knowing full well that it would be used as a cemetery for Protestants. In doing so, he ran the risk of being involved in serious trouble with Goa for having broken so important a territorial rule, and with the Bishop, who would face responsibility before his superiors for not having prevented the breaking of so important an ecclesiastical rule.

The conclusion of Manuel Pereira and the Governor that the only possible course was to sell the land to the East India Company was sound and well-evaluated. Someone had to break a rule. If the Bishop broke the rule, and allowed Protestants to be buried on Catholic soil, he would have the hounds of heaven after him. The thing would quite easily reach Rome. If the Governor broke the rule about land, it would not reach further than Goa, and he would be able to argue it out. As to the land being used as a cemetery for Protestants, in the peculiar condition of its being the only non-Portuguese parcel of land in the whole of Macao—all foreign property was rented—it could rationally be argued that the owners, being in a unique position, could take unique opportunity of it.

The Portuguese live beneath a weightier encrustation of law than probably any other European people. As they themselves say, and as the foregoing shows, there is a way round a law, but it has to be taken with thought for others—in this case, the Bishop.

Once the cemetery was properly laid out, a number of bodies of Britons, Dutchmen, Americans, and others interred without the walls were transferred within. The earliest tombstone date in the cemetery is for this reason earlier than the date of the cemetery's foundation.

In 1833, by an Act of Parliament passed at Westminster, the East India Company lost its monopoly of British trade with China. The monopoly had been fundamentally eroded by private British traders, to restrict whom would merely serve to increase the trade of Americans and other rivals. Not dissimilar from earlier Portuguese experience, the East India Company had become an Elizabethan anachronism. It could not continue except under the conditions in which it was founded—national monopoly, which had ceased to exist. It was decided in Calcutta and London to close down the Company's establishment in China.

The Casa Garden, vacated by the Company in 1835, was occupied for a short period by the Dents, who headed a leading British opium firm—all concerns of any stability in those days were opium firms. Manuel Pereira then gave it to his daughter, as part of her wedding gift. Part of . . . they were extremely wealthy.

Pereira's son-in-law, Commendador Lourenço Marques, was an enthusiast of the Camões tradition. During his occupancy of the mansion and garden, around the beginning of the opium War, the trees and walks around the Rocks of Camões were improved, and a bust of the poet was installed (1840) under a somewhat inappropriate classical canopy. Much in keeping with the times—it was the age of romantic ruins—Marques called it the Grotto of Camoens—*a gruta de Camões*—a name that has lamentably stuck. He next introduced a visitors' book, in which well-known people coming to Macao were invited to write, if they felt so inclined, on the subject of Camões in the context of Macao.

Many eminent persons visiting the Far East, from British royalty onwards, were received by the Marques family, and he soon had a varied collection of poems of tribute to Camões in several languages, including French, Spanish, Latin, and Chinese. Then, in 1849, the scholarly John Bowring, one of the foremost English intellectuals of the time, later to become Governor of Hongkong, contributed a sonnet in English. Marques was so delighted with this—it is a charming poem, completely capturing the atmosphere of the place—that it led to a further development at the 'grotto'. Bowring's sonnet, and a selection of the better poems in the visitors' book, were carved in stone and fixed into the rocks surrounding the poet's bust.

In 1866 the original bust, which had been damaged by vandals, was replaced by a bronze designed by a leading Lisbon sculptor, Bordalo Pinheiro. The attractive rocks, with their huge overhanging trees, had become a unique international memorial and tribute to the poet; and thus they have remained. The entire property passed into the hands of the state in 1886, the offending canopy was removed, and further improvements followed, aimed at keeping the whole in its natural aspect.

Considering that Camoes' tomb in Lisbon is empty, and that nearly 300 years passed before he was commemorated in the Jerónimos, it could be said that his true monument is this one in Macao, with its unbroken tradition of his sojourn there.

The Opium War

The period during which Macao was the outpost of all Europe in China—with equal justice it could be called the British period, and often is—ended amid the alarms and uncertainties of the Opium War (1830–42).

One would assume that these must have been critical years for the city, and in the sense that one false move and all would be lost, they were. But there were no false moves, thus it would be truer to say these were exciting years, during which, with great skill, Macao walked a tightrope—the kind of excitement experienced before and after the event, not during it. Macao during these years was saved by the Governor, and by its own people.

From the moment the East India Company lost its monopoly, sounding the gong for a free-for-all among the British traders, every thinking Portuguese in Macao realized it was simply a matter of time before there was a head-on clash between Britain and China, and that it was imperative Macao keep out of it if she was not to be the first fatality. Fortunately, in Adrião Accacio da Silveira Pinto she had an exceptionally clear-sighted Governor, shrewd and prudent, who saw the situation as his people did, and enjoyed their complete confidence. This last was doubly important in that Silveira Pinto's diplomatic moves were so finely judged, and had to be kept secret, that there were often moments when no one knew exactly what was happening, and could not be told till later. The people's confidence was vital in such circumstances.

Years earlier, the Portuguese had cursed the British for strangling them out of the opium trade. In that the coming clash would almost certainly be on the issue of opium, people now saw that it had in fact been a blessing in disguise. Macao was truthfully able to tell the Chinese she was not involved in the opium trade. In fact, it was a physical impossibility not to be involved in some degree. When the crisis came, Silveira Pinto ordered that all godowns and warehouses be emptied of opium, and the 3,000 chests so declared were shipped off to Manila.

The immediate outcome of the abolition of the East India Company's monopoly was a staggering increase in the volume of the opium trade. Already very large, the trade doubled in five years. Meanwhile from Peking came persistent rumours that the Emperor Tao Kuang (1821–50) was contemplating some kind of restrictive action, possibly drastic.

These rumours proved to be true. Late in January 1839 it was learned that the Emperor had appointed one of the provincial viceroys, Lin Tse-hsü, to be Imperial High Commissioner, embodied with imperial powers, to stamp out the opium trade, utterly and for ever. The greatest and most sudden drop in prices ever recorded took place. Even the Calcutta market stagnated. In March the Imperial High Commissioner arrived in Canton, ordered the surrender of all opium for destruction, and when the British were recalcitrant, besieged them in their 'factories', depriving them of food and water, and preventing their escape. When all the opium—more than 20,000 chests of it—had finally been surrendered and destroyed, the foreigners were allowed to leave, and re-assembled in Macao.

News of the siege of the factories—it lasted six weeks—when it reached London, stirred public opinion on the theme of British lives in danger, and shortly afterwards a powerful British naval and military force headed for China. Though

London did not know it, war had already broken out there, in November 1839, with naval action in the Pearl River, in which a Chinese squadron was crippled by two British frigates.

Captain Charles Elliot, a naval officer who was in the anomalous position of being superintendent of British trade with China, was determined that the only possible course for British merchants was to abandon all thought of ever returning to Canton, and in future conduct their trade entirely through Macao. He offered the Macao government as much credit as it needed to put the settlement in a full state of defence. He suggested arming a number of vessels to act as coastguards, and that in the event of siege by the Chinese there should be arrangements to provision the city directly from Manila. In such an eventuality, Elliot stated, British subjects could by his authority be at the Governor's disposal for the protection of Macao in the interests of the Portuguese Crown.

Silveira Pinto liked Elliot—everyone except the British opium merchants liked him—but he had no faith in Britain's long-term disposition, nor did he deem it wise for Macao so to depart from her traditional relationship with the Chinese as to do something she had never in all her history done—arm herself against them. Nor did he think this would succeed. He replied to Elliot, saying he considered he must maintain neutrality as long as he could.

This was not only the correct decision, but a courageous one. Activity at the barrier gate was stepping up towards one of the immemorial food blockades which had invariably brought the city to its knees, while Lin Tse-hsü intimated to Silveira Pinto privately that he might wish to take over Macao's forts and announced a visit.

The situation was so grave that the Governor finally informed the British that unless their entire community left the place within eighteen hours, he could no longer be responsible for their safety. Every Briton, man, woman, and child, left, and took refuge in a large concourse of British merchant ships that were sheltering in Hongkong harbour. Three days later, the Imperial High Commission paid his official visit to Macao, the most powerful Chinese official ever to set foot in it. Silveira Pinto had already completed his display of friendliness to the British by handing the ladies aboard. With equal friendliness he now welcomed the formidable Lin.

The British found shipboard life in Hongkong so uncomfortable that, after Lin had gone, quite a number of them came back. Meanwhile, as an outcome of the state of war, Macao streets were plastered with Chinese official notices inciting Chinese to murder all Britons. When Captain Smith, who had commanded the naval encounter with which the war started, heard about the notices, he sailed a frigate into Macao's inner harbour to effect another British evacuation. This threw Silveira Pinto and the Senate into the highest alarms. The frigate was refused all facilities, and Smith was told to leave instantly, lest he put his countrymen into even greater danger than they were in already.

When Lin Tse-hsü discovered that no Britons in Macao had been murdered, he threatened to send an army to drive them out; and in these circumstances no Portuguese objections were raised when, in August 1840, Captain Smith sailed an armed steamer near the barrier gate, and landed some British troops north of it. After a short engagement, in which he completely routed the Chinese soldiery, he destroyed the barrier buildings and barracks, in full view of thousands of Macao spectators, who mounted the hills to watch.

Apart from this, Macao saw little of the war. In January 1841 the British flag was hoisted on the barren slopes of Hongkong Island, and in June the first auction of land there was held. Thereafter, in a gentle, imperceptible, yet steadily continuing movement, the vital element in Macao's population, which had made it one of the world's most significant cities, quietly drained away. In August 1842, with British troops poised for a full assault on Nanking, the dismayed and wrathful Emperor capitulated. Hongkong was formally ceded to the British Crown, and Canton, Amoy, Foochow, Ningpo, and Shanghai were declared open to foreign residence, Britons to reside there under their own laws, immune to Chinese jurisdiction.

Nor was it only the foreigners who left at the call of these new opportunities. Many Portuguese left as well. Nor were they only of the poorer sort. A number of them were from Macao's oldest and best-established families; and this tendency of the well-to-do to leave increased as it was seen how as opportunity augmented in the new settlements it dwindled in Macao.

It is, in fact, difficult to envisage how the new settlements could have functioned without the Portuguese, in particular because of their command of the Chinese language. When the Hongkong secretariat consisted of three men in a tent on the beach, one of the three men was a Portuguese, and it was much the same throughout. Numbers of Macao people founded their own firms, particularly in Hongkong, and still more took service as clerks in government and commerce. Until well into the present century, the government of Hongkong and the principal firms and banks in Hongkong and Shanghai were dependent for their smooth running on their methodical, painstaking Portuguese clerks, originally from Macao. Printing, the only form of manual labour the Macanese ever took to, became a virtual Portuguese monopoly in Hongkong and Shanghai, and remained so for the best part of 100 years.

One foreigner, however, did not leave. This was the artist George Chinnery, who had lived in Macao since 1825, painting while there all the pictures which have assured his fame, including the striking self-portrait in London's National Portrait Gallery. Chinnery paid one visit to Hongkong, in 1846. It was broiling summer, he was in his seventies, and did not feel at all well. After doing some vivid sketches of the place, he returned thankfully to Macao, and remained there till his death in 1852.

7

Sovereignty

Andrew Ljungstedt and Macao history

On 24 August 1841, Captain Elliot, the founder of Hongkong, boarded his ship of departure in Macao. He was accompanied by Commodore Bremer, who had been his commander-in-chief. Elliot's acquisition of Hongkong had been ridiculed by the British, and he himself dismissed by Lord Palmerston. Time was to vindicate Elliot's wisdom and judgment in accepting Hongkong when it was offered to him, though this seemed far from likely on that depressing day. Neither his successor, Sir Henry Pottinger, nor any of the more consequential Britons in China were present to see him off. His departure was ignored by all save the Portuguese. As he boarded his ship, one of the Macao forts fired a thirteen-gun salute.

The Portuguese had a good deal of sympathy with Elliot. Both they and he had received much the same treatment from the general run of the British community. The relations between the British and the Portuguese were now to take a more serious turn, at least from the Portuguese point of view. Macao, with its shallow, silted harbours, unsuited to modern shipping, was not only to become an economic backwater. It was to find itself in an inferior position in respect of its international status. When the terms of the Treaty of Nanking became known, it was found that the British had acquired sovereign rights over Hongkong.

The Portuguese had always claimed they had sovereign rights in Macao. Foreigners found their insistence on this point tiresome, indeed ridiculous, since it seemed to be so patently at variance with actual conditions. The Chinese customs office in

Macao was commercially the operative factor, not the Portuguese customs office. For years a Chinese watch force had patrolled the streets at night, and it was the operative factor in terms of law and order, not the Portuguese watch force. Whenever the magistrate of Chinshan, the sub-district immediately north of Macao, wished to arrest someone in the city, he ordered the Portuguese to do it for him, and if they did not obey (they usually did obey) he sent his men into the city to enforce compliance. On one occasion, when a Briton had caused a disturbance *in Canton*, the Chinshan magistrate ordered the Portuguese to throw the offender into gaol in Macao, and into gaol he went. How, foreigners asked, did all this equate with sovereign rights? Why did the Portuguese always obey?

They obeyed, of course, because they knew that if they did not, the entire Chinese population would be ordered to leave, and food supplies would be cut off. They would be starved into obedience. The sole item of nourishment Macao produced was well water.

It was useless, however, to ask questions of the Portuguese about these matters. They had sovereign rights.

Recently the issue had been brought uncomfortably to the fore by the publication of a history of Macao, the first ever written, by Andrew Ljungstedt, published in Boston in 1836. Ljungstedt, as a member of the Swedish Company, had been in Macao in 1802 when, in the interests of Macao's defence during the Napoleonic War, the Marquess Wellesley, Governor-General of India, had sent British troops to reinforce the garrison, warning the Governor that if he did not peaceably acquiesce in this, the troops would occupy the place by force. The tone of Wellesley's letter was so threatening that the Governor took the unprecedented step of sending an urgent message to Peking, asking that Macao be placed under the Emperor's personal protection.

Nothing came of it, because the Select Committee advised against the landing, and their opinion was accepted. But it set Ljungstedt thinking. Exactly what rights did the Portuguese have, and how had they come by them? After the Swedish Company closed down, he returned as honorary Consul for Sweden, and spent nearly ten years assembling material for his history, with the help of two local scholars who had access to the archives. Needless to say, he found nothing about sovereign rights.

Ljungstedt had a low opinion of the Portuguese, and made no effort to disguise the fact in his book, in which he inveighed against Macao's pious attitudinizing, its shallow pretence to sovereignty, its boasts, and double standards. But when Britain acquired sovereign rights by treaty, Ljungstedt's book made it awkwardly clear that while Hongkong was held by right, Macao was held on sufferance. The Portuguese, of course, still claimed they had sovereign rights, and from now on it became a prime concern of theirs to clarify the matter. Urgency was given to it by the number of other nations which now proceeded to sign treaties with China.

American and French treaties with China

Although during the Opium War the Americans had given the British little help, save delivering merchants' cargoes, and the French had actually been in negotiation with the Chinese in Canton to assist with ships and arms against the British, these two nations swiftly took advantage of British success.

In February 1844, Caleb Cushing reached Macao as American Minister, with powers to conclude a treaty with China, his instructions being to obtain for Americans the same rights at the Treaty Ports as enjoyed by the British. He had also to deliver a letter to the Emperor from the President of the United States, John Tyler. As the British were at this time themselves negotiating with the Chinese for the Treaty Ports to be open to all nations, Cushing's mission was narrowed to the problem of how to avoid being treated as a tribute-bearing barbarian envoy.

When he announced to the Governor of Kwangtung and Kwangsi that his orders were to proceed to Peking, he was quickly informed that a reverent memorial would have to be sent first, requesting permission. In fact, within a few weeks he found himself locked in the same coils as all former foreign plenipotentiaries. Baffled, and beginning to lose his temper in the immemorial way, he was only saved from deserting the pacific aim of his mission by the timely information that Kiying, the high Manchu official who had recently ratified the Treaty of Nanking had been appointed Governor of Kwangtung, and was shortly coming southward to negotiate a treaty with him.

Cushing's house in Macao, the home of a former governor, became the first American Legation in China. Two weeks after reaching Canton, Kiying came to Macao to meet Cushing, and took residence for the duration of the treaty talks in the temple of Kwan Yin at Mong Ha, between which and the American Legation formal visits were exchanged. But when Cushing pressed for permission to go to Peking to present his letter at an imperial audience, Kiying simply replied that if the envoy persisted in this, the talks would have to be discontinued. Finally, Cushing handed the President's letter to Kiying for transmission to the Emperor; and on 3 July, on a stone table in a forecourt of the temple, the Treaty of Wanghia (Mong Ha) was signed.

The French followed the same course. Their envoy, Théodose de Lagrené, came to Macao in August 1844, and signed a treaty on board a French ship at Whampoa the following October. Under the terms of this treaty the Emperor issued edicts tolerating Christianity, and restoring property formerly seized from Catholic missions. Belgium acquired formal permission from Peking to trade under the existing treaties (1845), and in 1847 China concluded a treaty with Sweden.

The rights which these nations peacefully obtained were those gained by the British in war. The British not having pressed for a permanent representative in Peking—their Minister in China was also Governor of Hongkong, where his services were more or less continually required—the French and American diplomatic missions were not allowed in Peking, and had to take residence, *faute de mieux*, in Macao. While most of the erstwhile foreign community was leaving to set themselves up in Hongkong or Shanghai, this influx of diplomats, which included the accredited representatives of Spain, Brazil, and Peru, lent its distinctive colour to Macao society during the next twenty years.

Minor concessions to Macao—friction with Hongkong

The Portuguese too tried to improve their status. While Kiying was in South China for the ratification of the Treaty of Nanking (Hongkong, 1843), a despatch was sent to him by the Governor of Macao, asking for the abolition of the ground rent and many of the other frustrating restrictions placed on the settlement through the centuries. The request was referred to Peking, from which an answer was received, dated April 1844.

The only concessions made were that from henceforth the Senate might address the Chinshan magistrate on terms of equality—he was too low in the Chinese hierarchy to matter—and the permits and fees required for new buildings and repairs were waived. The Chinese customs office remained where it was; ground rent was still demanded; Chinese jurisdiction in Macao was still maintained by right.

Even these small concessions were probably made under the fear that, if the Portuguese were not satisfied, the British would come to their assistance. Actually the British, once

Hongkong began to show signs of life, and trade at Shanghai was flourishing, paid no more attention to the Portuguese. Macao had served their purpose. Although it was pleasant for the older generation of Hongkong merchants to have their summer residences in Macao, and the place had its sentimental attractions, these did not constitute any reason why the British should bestir themselves to assist it in any way.

With their difficulty at grasping inter-barbarian relationships, the Chinese, failing to appreciate this, continued to suppose the ties between British and Portuguese to be closer than they really were. Had they been more acute in this respect, they would have noticed, as early as 1844, the antipathies which could easily be aroused between the two.

In that year, the Hongkong legislature passed an ordinance whereby, consequent on the extraterritorial arrangements under the Treaty of Nanking, the laws of Great Britain were made to apply to all British subjects in China, including Macao. The wording of the ordinance was tactless—the first draft stated that Macao was 'deemed and taken to be within the dominions of the emperor of China'—and it caused a storm of indignation, accusation, and protests on both sides of the Pearl River, ending with an exchange between Lisbon and London, in which Lord Aberdeen, the Foreign Secretary, endeavoured to explain the Hongkong ordinance, but gave no assurance that it would be altered.

The law meant that should a British subject be arrested and charged for any offence committed in China, or Macao, he must be surrendered for trial in the courts of Hongkong, or by such courts as British consuls at treaty ports were entitled to convene. On the grounds that such a law prevented Europeans being tried by the too summary laws of China, the Macanese had no objection to it. But in Macao there were Portuguese courts, and it was in relation to these that the new law was considered an affront to national dignity.

Amaral's measures to reduce Chinese interference

After the failure to obtain greater rights from the Chinese, the government in Lisbon grew restive about the situation. It was thought that a strong and determined governor, with the aid of the existing garrison, would, in the new circumstances created by China's defeat in war, be able to remove by force what the Chinese declined to yield in parley. Observing, furthermore, that the quick growth of Hongkong was due to its being a free port, the Minister for the Colonies decided that Macao too should be free. The Governor, José Gregorio Pegado (1843–6), warned Lisbon that Macao as a free port would lose her most important source of revenue—customs dues—but his advice was ignored.

The man chosen to put this bold but ill-considered policy into effect was João Maria Ferreira do Amaral, a captain in the Portuguese Navy with a distinguished record of active service, in the course of which—in South America in 1823—he lost his right arm. Taking office as Governor in 1846, Amaral was ordered to assert Portugal's absolute sovereignty in the settlement. Since no additional naval or military forces were sent to assist him in this, the Senate, seeing only one of the classic food blockades coming, with further humiliations to follow, was opposed to his policy from the start.

Amaral, however, was an officer of the greatest resolution, and in his firm proceedings with the Chinese he was to some extent encouraged by the similar attitude adopted by the British, in regard to the continued refusal of the authorities at Canton to open the city to foreign residents. There had been no such trouble in the other Treaty Ports. Canton alone remained obdurate.

Negotiations between Hongkong's Governor, Sir John Davis, and Kiying having failed to produce any improvement, in April

1847 Major-General G. C. D'Aguilar, commander-in-Chief at Hongkong, led a British force up the river, and within thirty-six hours, having assaulted and taken all the principal forts from the rivermouth to Canton, occupied the foreign factories, the enclave in which alone foreigners were allowed.

This was little more than a vulgar demonstration of force, but it produced an effect. Kiying formally agreed with Davis that after two years, during which it was hoped the Cantonese would become accustomed to the new situation and be less hostile to foreigners, the city would be opened.

Amaral carefully associated himself with the British as far as possible. He and Davis exchanged formal visits. When a Chinese riot broke out in Macao, in protest against new taxation introduced to replace the revenue lost by the closure of the Portuguese customs office, Amaral asked for a British warship to be sent to Macao to evacuate citizens wishing to leave, should the situation further deteriorate. Davis met this request at once, and H.M.S. *Vulture* remained in Macao waters while the disorders lasted.

Having put down the riot, Amaral issued a conciliatory proclamation to the Chinese, whose answer was to shut all their shops and stop bringing provisions into the city. With the British warship standing by, Amaral replied that unless within twenty-four hours all the shops were open and the market full of provisions, the guns of the Monte would open fire on the market area, and raze all its buildings to the ground. The following morning, riding past the market, he found everything in its usual bustle and animation.

Amaral saw clearly the Macao he wanted, and with admirable assessment of the Chinese character, he proceeded towards it by a sequence of reforms, beginning with the least serious. Marine licensing was improved, and brought more under Portuguese authority. Cantonese landowners between the

117

city wall and the barrier were made liable to taxation by the Macao government, while it was stated that so far as Macao was concerned, such landholders were under no obligation to pay taxes to the Chinese authorities. (It was the Chinese, after all, who had placed the barrier gate where it was, more than a mile from the city.)

A small post of the Chinese customs which had for generations exacted landing fees on the Praia Grande, within a hundred yards of the Governor's palace, was forcibly closed down, and the officer in charge—there was some likelihood that he was not an officer at all, but the descendant of a family who had been posing as customs officers for over a century— was ordered to be out of Macao within twenty-four hours. Kiying made a formal objection, to which Amaral replied in a very civil letter, pointing out that as Queen Maria II had declared Macao to be a free port, there was no necessity for customs officers to be posted there. It was a hint of what he had in mind for the future: the closure of the main Chinese customs office.

In recent years, the fields and low hills between the city and the barrier had become so popular with Chinese as a burial place that there was hardly an uncultivated acre that was not littered with tombs. In view of the city's rising population, it was necessary to extend the town beyond the walls, and, to avoid the dangers of disease and fire, clean up the shack area under the walls. Above all, a proper road was required, connecting the city with the barrier gate, to improve the absurd position whereby goods had to be borne in along small tracks through a network of smallholdings and tombs. Without fear of Chinese reactions, Amaral ordered the removal of graves as required for these works, offering compensation to poor families.

Knowing the extreme Chinese anger this would arouse, the Senate secretly petitioned the Minister for the Colonies concerning the danger of this anti-Chinese policy. When he discovered this, Amaral disbanded the Senate, and published the full details in the government bulletin, branding the Senators as unpatriotic. Amid growing Chinese discontent and the hostility of his own people, he continued his administration under what amounted to martial law.

Finally, on 5 March 1849, he issued a proclamation ordering the closure of the Chinese customs house. When this was ignored, he ordered the entire Chinese customs staff to leave the city. He also informed the Chinshan magistrate that in future Chinese officers entering Macao would receive the honours accorded to visiting representatives of foreign powers.

Though the customs staff departed without protest, it was evident within a few days that pressure was being brought on Chinese merchants, landowners, and cultivators to leave the city, with the intention of diverting all its normal trade to Whampoa. Amaral responded by ordering that if any merchant or landowner left without a written permit from the procurator's office, his land and possessions would be deemed forfeit to the Crown. Not even this prevented a steady exodus of Chinese throughout the summer, during which the resolute Governor held his own, surrounded on every side by prophecies of downfall.

April 1849 was the month scheduled in Kiying's agreement with Sir John Davis for the opening of Canton city to foreigners. Amaral's measures against the Chinese customs office were timed to coincide with what was expected to be another British demonstration in the river. Slightly in advance of the date, Davis' successor, George Bonham (Governor of Hongkong 1848–54) raised the subject with Kiying's successor, Hsü Kuang-tsin. The attitude of the Canton populace had not changed, and as Hsü candidly stated in his reply, in defiance of the obvious wishes of the people the new measure could not be introduced.

Palmerston, who was again in office in England, had advised Bonham against resorting to hostilities to obtain this right which, were it granted, might be impossible for British subjects to enjoy in the face of Cantonese hatred and violence. As a result, when Hsü's refusal was received, Bonham did nothing. The Chinese were jubilant. Hsü was promoted, and the incident was regarded as a victory.

Amaral's position in Macao was weakened by this, but not destroyed. The cordial relations he maintained with Bonham were known to the Chinese, who were far from certain whether, were Macao openly threatened, the Governor of Hongkong would not be aroused to create a disturbance. What was also known was that Amaral alone stood in the way of Macao subsiding into its former humility toward the Celestial Empire.

A Protestant at Corpus Christi

In June, British and American warships and other craft took part in a regatta at Macao. Among the civilian passengers, they brought with them one James Summers, a teacher at St. Paul's College, Hongkong. The day before the regatta, 7th June, was the feast of Corpus Christi. Summers, curious to see the idolatrous rites of the Catholic Church on this occasion, stationed himself at a good vantage point in one of the streets through which the procession was to pass, in which the Governor and all the principal dignitaries of Macao would participate.

Conforming with custom, every man removed his hat as the Host approached. Summers however, as a teacher in the principal Protestant school in Hongkong, did not consider himself under any obligation to remove his hat. When others with him, also from Hongkong, warned him to take it off, he ignored them; and being in a good position to see, he was seen. One of the priests walking before the Host asked him to uncover, and since he again took no notice, signalled him out to Amaral, who was walking just behind. An orderly was sent, demanding that Summers take his hat off, shortly after which, with his hat still on, he was arrested. The procession passed on to the church, Summers to the common gaol.

From there he wrote, asking for help, to one of the naval officers, who, with the senior British officer, Captain Henry Keppel, waited on Amaral the following morning to ask for Summers' release. Amaral, in conversation, justified the arrest on the two counts of offering insult to the religion of the State and disobeying an order by the Governor, but agreed that if Keppel was requesting the man's release as a favour, he would ask the judge for clemency. Keppel in reply asked for no favour. He demanded release as a right, under the Hongkong ordinance including Macao within the Emperor of China's dominions. Amaral was left with no alternative, for the honour of the Portuguese Crown, but to refuse.

The regatta started as arranged. As soon as Amaral, who was to witness it from an American warship, was clear of the city, Keppel took the law into his own hands. A British officer was sent in plain clothes to visit Summers, in order to find out exactly how to reach him. On his return, a small, well-armed party of marines was sent ashore. Landing on the Praia Grande, within a stone's throw of the Governor's palace, the men quickly advanced to the Senate House just inland, at the back of which was the civil prison. Overpowering a sentry, they entered the prison, shot dead an unarmed private who gave the alarm, and, against the resistance of the aroused guard, three of whom were wounded, rushed Summers out of the building and down into their boat, all in the space of a few minutes.

When the Governor returned in the afternoon, and was informed of what had happened, he ordered the forts to be manned and the guns trained on the British ships. Only as his anger cooled somewhat was he persuaded against giving the final order to them to open fire. Instead, formal protests were delivered, via the Governor of Hongkong to Lord Palmerston, and from the Portuguese Minister for Foreign Affairs to the British Minister in Lisbon. After considerable press comment in London and Lisbon, Palmerston gave a formal apology, censured Keppel, and pensioned the family of the dead Portuguese soldier.

Assassination of Amaral

There, among the Europeans, the matter rested, all the correct gestures having been made. But, for the Chinese, the sight of Macao's guns aligned on British warships was a revelation of something hitherto unsuspected. The Summers incident, with the anger and high-flown talk it aroused in Macao, showed for the first time the shallowness of the friendship between British and Portuguese. In other words, it was now considered safe to strike.

Within a few weeks, the same kind of public notices as had been issued by Lin Tse-Tsü during the Opium War were posted in the streets of Canton, offering rewards for Amaral's head. For several weeks the notices appeared, while the restiveness of the Macao Chinese increased. Amaral, who sensed that his assassination was a matter of time, continued his accustomed way of living. On 22 August 1849 he rode out to the barrier. It was one of his usual routes. Near the barrier was an aged and disabled Chinese woman who lived on his charity. When, that afternoon, one of his Chinese servants warned him not to go, he paid no attention.

After giving money to the woman, he was passing a beach on his way back to Macao, accompanied by an aide-de-camp, when a Chinese boy ran out and struck him on the face with a light bamboo stick. The horses reared, and as Amaral turned towards the boy, seven men burst from an ambush and attacked him with short-swords. Putting the reins between his teeth, the one-armed Governor drew his sword and defended himself proudly. His aide-de-camp, unhorsed, disarmed and slightly wounded, fled. Thrown by his horse, Amaral fought in the sand with his assailants until one of them, with a dexterous blow, severed his only hand. Holding the bleeding body down in the sand, they then hacked off its head, and with this and the hand, made off into the countryside, away to Canton to claim their money.

When the horrified Macanese, proud of their Governor's magnificent end, and ashamed of their former complaints against him, came to carry home his lacerated remains, it was noticed that the Chinese barrier post and barracks were deserted. It seemed to suggest that the guards might be party to the design, and three Chinese soldiers, found after a search, were accordingly arrested. A council was set up, consisting of a bishop, judge, and senior army officer, to administer the government. As night fell, tension mounted in the Chinese quarters, and the following morning Chinese levies could be seen massing north of the barrier. The assassination, it appeared, was the item in a plan to terrorize the city.

Mesquita—Pak Shan Lan

For once, however, Macao was not friendless. The Governor's death provoked horror and sympathy among the entire foreign community on the China coast. John W. Davis, the American Commissioner, immediately authorized two warships to be stationed at Macao in case of need, while from Hongkong came two British frigates, despatched by Bonham as soon as he heard the report. Bonham, Davis, Baron Forth-Rouen, the French envoy, and the Spanish envoy Sinibaldo de Mas, sent letters to the Governor of Kwangtung, expressing their disgust at the crime.

The Macao Council had sent without delay to the Chinshan magistrate, demanding the return of Amaral's head and hand, but had received no answer. As Chinese forces in the vicinity increased, a clamour arose among the Portuguese for offensive action. Portuguese senior officers advised prudence, but many local people dismissed this as unrealistic, saying that the moment Chinese troops advanced, the Cantonese mob in Macao itself would rise, to prevent which the prudent course would be for Macao to take the initiative.

On 25 August, the day after the men-of-war arrived, the young Macanese aide-de-camp to the Council, Lieutenant Vicente Nicolau de Mesquita, asked if he might have the Council's permission to disregard the restraining orders of his commanding officer. With a small force of picked men, he wished to storm the fort of Pak Shan Lan, about a mile beyond the barrier gate, where Chinese forces were concentrating.

Permission was given, though very reluctantly—the Council did not wish to lose its side, and the mission was foolhardy. By the time Mesquita reached the barrier, the Chinese had already opened fire on the Portuguese soldiers defending it, prelude to a full assault. Producing his warrant from the Council, Mesquita informed his commanding officer that he proposed to take the city's one howitzer—the gift of a French naval commander to Amaral—out beyond the barrier, to within range of Pak Shan Lan fort. With sixteen men he went forward, loaded the howitzer in the face of Chinese gunfire, and with his first shot hit the centre of the fort, causing a large number of deaths and a general scare among the Chinese troops.

The shot, however, broke the howitzer's mechanism, which could not be repaired. Mesquita therefore went back, and again producing for his superior a warrant from the Council, asked for twenty more men to accompany him to storm the fort. The required number having volunteered, with thirty-six men in all the young ensign advanced, leading them in single file through the rice fields. From the hills, many hundreds of Macao people watched as the file, moving with interminable slowness against the gunfire and beneath the glare of the year's hottest sun, advanced on what was suspected to be several hundred Chinese soldiers in the fort. The foreign representatives watched from Monte fort. It was like a display of skill and strength in an unreal, deathly circus. The spectators could only postulate that Mesquita and his men were walking to their death. From the Chinese side, another 2,000 local levies, additional to those in the fort, watched from various nearby vantages.

As the Macanese neared the fort, the Chinese guns, adjusted to fire into the distance, no longer covered them, so that for several crucial yards they were able to advance more speedily and with impunity. When they were within range of the soldiers on the walls, the Macanese opened fire with their rifles, keeping it up as they mounted the slope to the battlements.

Although almost every shot fired took the life of a soldier, it cannot have been this alone that produced the next reaction of the defenders. Perhaps it seemed to them that the thirty-six must be endowed with supernatural powers, that they could pass unhurt through such a cannonade, and still dare attack so many adversaries. More likely, the majority were recruits with no military training, and no discipline. Whatever the cause, even before Mesquita reached the walls, there was confusion within. As the Macanese soldiers topped the fortifications, some of the Chinese were already stampeding to escape, while others, in despair, were on the point of exploding the powder magazine, in order to atone by suicide, according to Chinese military honour, for the disgrace of defeat.

By keeping up a death-dealing fire around all those attempting to come near the magazine, the Macanese saved themselves from being involved in a holocaust, nor did they spare any their shots could reach in the terror-stricken mêlée before them. Instead, the incredible happened. In utter disorder, the garrison fled. As though they feared the presence of ghostly elements, they even dragged all their casualties with them, the wounded and the dead. When the Portuguese flag, which one of the heroes had optimistically carried under his shirt, rose fluttering from the ramparts, long and frenzied cheering broke out among the spectators on the Monte, from which the flag was just visible in the distance.

The evident excitement in the Monte, with people rushing out to tell the glad tidings, was misinterpreted by those on the town side as a sign of disaster. British troops landed, expecting to be called upon to defend the city or cover an evacuation. When messengers at last brought the report of victory, the incredulous citizens streamed out by hundreds to give Mesquita and his men a triumphal welcome. Before retiring from Pak Shan Lan, the storming party spiked the Chinese guns in the fort, and having severed the head and hand of one of the only bodies left—that of an officer—they bore these grisly trophies aloft to Macao. Finally, they blew the fort up.

In the tense days that followed, British marines marched out to the deserted barrier; the British and American warships remained at Macao; by arrangement with the French envoy, a detachment of French troops reinforced the garrison; and the Spanish envoy urgently requested the despatch of several gunboats from Manila. These firmly concerted measures, added to Mesquita's spectacular sortie, put an end to Chinese interference in Macao—for more than a century, as it turned out. The barrier guardroom and barracks were dismantled and replaced by a Portuguese post, provided with defensive cover by two forts constructed on nearby hills within the barrier, the forts of Mong Ha and Dona Maria II.

Yet though Governor Hsü might no longer dare argue about Chinese rights in Macao, he still held the head and hand of Amaral, over which, in correspondence with the Portuguese, he proceeded to argue for more than four months, during which time the body of the dead governor lay unburied in his palace. Hsü's claim was that, the murderer of Amaral having been apprehended and executed, the Portuguese had no right to detain any longer the three soldiers arrested at the barrier after the assassination. Macao's reply was that there was more than one assassin, that the soldiers were clearly implicated in the plot to kill Amaral, and they were only prepared to surrender them if the head and hand were returned promptly.

Hsü, however, who had lost face, had no intention of being reasonable. In December the Portuguese gave in, and returned the three prisoners; and in January 1850, when, on a given day, a large concourse of people assembled on the Praia Grande to honour the return of the governor's remains, Hsü completed his revenge. Instead of the expected mandarin boat with an escort, a small hired craft drew up, with two low-ranking watch force men bearing the head and hand in a pig basket.

Abortive invasion of Canton—gambling
The principal aim of Portuguese policy towards China now became to obtain *de jure* the sovereignty over Macao that the storming of Pak Shan Lan seemed to have already given them *de facto*. This policy was set in motion in 1850 with a somewhat unrealistic project to invade Canton and, in British fashion, dictate a Sino-Portuguese treaty.

An extraordinary series of disasters and mishaps sterilized the invasion. Troops to be sent from Portugal were not sent. Naval reinforcements arrived in a deplorable condition, the ships requiring extensive repairs before being fit to use in operations of war. Amaral's successor, Pedro Alexandrino da Cunha, arrived in May, but died after only thirty-eight days in office. The next Governor, Gonçalves Cardoso, who fell foul of the Macanese in the same way as Amaral, but in less heroic circumstances, was replaced after ten months. In October 1850 the flagship of the proposed invasion force, its main hope, blew up at Taipa with all hands aboard.

During the next governorship, that of Captain Isidoro Francisco Guimarães (1851–63), commander of the remaining cruiser sent for the invasion, Macao was again reduced to achieving its ends with the Chinese by peaceful negotiation, without any appreciable armed force. Guimarães and his successor, Coelho do Amaral, were two of Macao's best governors; and being unimpeded by Chinese interference, they between them laid the settled outlines of Macao as it is today.

In 1844, Macao, Timor, and Solor had been belatedly detached from Goa, and constituted a province. The islet of Solor, once rich in nutmeg, had been wrecked by the Dutch in their policy of destroying all spice-trees beyond range of their monopoly control, centred in Amboina. Solor had not only been ruined, but the Dutch had turned a blind eye when a fanatical Muslim sect from their territory massacred much of Solor's Christian population, and forcibly converted the rest. The islet was now Muslim. What remained of Portuguese Solor was the small settlement of Larantuka at the eastern end of Flores and the island of Adonara opposite. After a few years under Macao's shadowy jurisdiction, this whole area was exchanged for part of Dutch Timor.

As for Timor, once the unique source of sandalwood, over the centuries no one had replanted, and the island was now denuded of the precious tree. Portuguese Timor proved a constant drain on Macao's slender resources.

To support Timor, and to assure Macao a measure of internal financial stability, Guimarães now introduced what has become the most widely known feature of contemporary Macao—licensed gambling. The innovation was markedly successful from the outset, financially as well as in terms of public order, the old unlicensed gambling houses, of which there were many, having been the traditional resort of Chinese bad characters. But it went further than this. It led to a remarkable improvement in the actual apprehension of criminals, the gambling 'farmer's' organization being a kind of auxiliary detective service. When searching for a wanted man, the police chief simply passed the details to the 'farmer', and within hours the culprit was in police custody. The improvement in public order and the prosecution of crime was so marked that Governor Guimarães privately suggested to Sir John Bowring, by this time Governor of Hongkong, that Hongkong too should introduce licensed gambling. A proposal to this effect was actually made to London, where Queen Victoria's Ministers viewed it with raised eyebrows and tight-lipped horror, saying that any such development was quite out of the question. Murderers thus continued to go scot-free in Hongkong, despite the existence of a large and expensive police force, while in Macao, with a mere handful of police, criminals knew they could not get away with it.

The licensed fantan saloons of Macao, frequented by all nationalities, including large numbers of weekend holidaymakers from Hongkong, gave the place the nocturnal reputation of being an oriental Monte Carlo, in curious contrast to its daytime appearance, which was predominantly that of a religious centre and quiet country port. Though Timor was later detached from Macao's administration, the gambling houses carried on, being by that time too valuable and regular a source of revenue to be dispensed with.

End of Macao's foreign community

In 1850 the long series of uprisings known generally as the Taiping Rebellion broke out in Kwangsi. Led by Hung Hsiu-Ch'uan who, with some crackpot ideas of Christianity, declared himself Prince of Heaven and the younger brother of Jesus, it introduced a confusing new issue into relations between Chinese and foreigners. In those parts of the country where the rebels were unpopular, people associated foreigners with them, as being fellow-Christians, and there was a spontaneous upsurge of anti-foreign feeling. Notices inciting people to kill all Europeans were posted in Canton and other cities, without government authority, and all foreigners, particularly missionaries working in remote rural areas, were in grave danger. The number of Protestant missionaries in Macao increased significantly, and the outbreak of the Second Anglo-Chinese War, which began with local hostilities in the Canton area in 1856, brought even more refugees to Macao.

In her second war with China, Great Britain was joined by France, and had the close support of the United States and Russia. Canton was occupied in 1858, after which the British and French plenipotentiaries, the Earl of Elgin and Baron Gros, negotiated treaties at Tientsin opening still more Chinese ports, and obtaining the right to station permanent diplomatic representatives in Peking. Thinking their work done, they then returned to Europe.

In April 1859, the first British Minister-designate to China, Frederick Bruce, younger brother of Lord Elgin, arrived in Hongkong, where he had formerly served as Colonial Secretary, and spent some days in Macao in consultation with the resident French Commissioner, de Bourboulon, who was to be Napoleon III's chargé d'affaires in China.

An opportunity of this kind was what Governor Guimarães had been hoping for. Taking advantage of his position as representative of their host-country, he openly solicited the help of the Ministers in obtaining a Sino-Portuguese treaty. With some embarrassment on all sides, he was fobbed off with the excuse that the Ministers already had on their hands as much as they could cope with.

Bruce sailed to the Peiho, and finding the mouth of the river blocked against him, was obliged to withdraw to Shanghai. War was resumed. Elgin and Gros returned to China, and with a powerful Anglo-French force, advanced to Peking, whence the Emperor Hsien Fêng (1849–61) fled to Jehol. Elgin and Gros entered the capital in state, exchanged the ratification of the Treaties of Tientsin, and signed a further Convention, in which China made more concessions, including the opening of Tientsin as a treaty port, and the cession of Kowloon to the British Crown.

In the years that followed, forces under European direction, operating from Shanghai, assisted the Chinese to stamp out the Taiping insurrection. By 1865 the first foreign legations were being established in Peking, and conditions throughout the country were improving sufficiently for most of the refugees in Macao (and Hongkong) to re-enter China. Within two years nearly the whole of Macao's foreign community left, the diplomats to Peking, the businessmen to the Treaty Ports or to the interior of the country (declared open for foreign travellers), the missionaries to their interior settlements and parishes.

A Sino-Portuguese treaty

At the first sign of this exodus, Guimarães rightly gauged that in negotiating a treaty, it was nearing the time of now or never. In 1862, with the necessary powers delegated to him by Lisbon, he travelled to Tientsin unheralded, and with French diplomatic assistance, concluded a treaty acknowledging Portuguese sovereignty over Macao. When, however, two years later, his successor, José Rodrigues Coelho do Amaral (1863–6), came to Tientsin to exchange the ratifications, the Chinese tried to introduce new clauses modifying those already agreed. Since to have negotiated further would have set a precedent of the type Chinese officials would batten on in the future, the Governor, following Elgin's stern example—and correct European procedure—declined any form of discussions, and withdrew to Macao, which for another twenty-two years subsisted as before, treatyless but uninterfered with.

Coelho Do Amaral, who was by profession a civil engineer, improved the city in many ways. Parts of the old city wall were demolished, and the insanitary shack areas near it were converted into decent Chinese commercial and residential quarters, thus beginning an expansion of the city proper northwards into the zone between the old walls and the barrier gate. Macadamized roads and streets lighting were introduced, and a programme of tree-planting was started. This painstaking governor's best memorial could be said to be the gnarled old trees along the Praia Grande which, together with the sea-wall and surfaced road, are all part of his conception. One is hardly conscious today that the city ever had walls. In fact, where streets and public gardens become rectilinear, Coelho do Amaral's city begins and the old city ends.

A combination of two issues at last led to a treaty with China. The first of these issues was international.

In the 1880s France entered her most aggressive period as an imperialist power in the East, advancing the Frontiers of her Indo-Chinese possessions to the southern limits of the Chinese Empire. In 1884–5 the French were at war with China, where they plainly intended to establish themselves as the principal foreign power. In Europe they instituted diplomatic moves for France to acquire Macao, Portugal to receive in exchange some territory in French Equatorial Africa. To the British, the prospect of the French in this expansive mood settling themselves as Hongkong's neighbour was not acceptable, and opportunity was sought to counter such a move.

The second of the two issues was local. Since the Second Anglo-Chinese War, the Chinese Imperial Maritime Customs had been reorganized under European direction, for the mutual benefit of foreign traders and of the slowly tottering Ch'ing dynasty. At the head of the customs was a Briton, Sir Robert Hart, who was at this time attempting to control the import of opium into China, Peking's policy having altered in this sense. In 1886 he succeeded in concluding with the Hongkong government an agreement, under which Hongkong would in future adopt control measures similar to those in force in the Treaty Ports, report movements of opium, and accept a Chinese customs post at Kowloon.

Hongkong, however, only agreed to cooperate provided it was guaranteed that Macao would do the same. To introduce control of opium in Hongkong only, after all, would throw the whole of lucrative trade into the hands of the Portuguese. It was thus made an item of the agreement with Hart that China would ask for Macao's cooperation. This at last put Macao in a bargaining position in its relations with China.

The talks began in Lisbon, where a protocol was drawn up between the Minister of Foreign Affairs and a representative of the Chinese Customs, who was of course British, not Chinese. By this convenient device, Sir Robert Hart was able to ensure, as if it were a Chinese proviso, that the item in which the British were interested, as a safeguard against French aims in South China, be included in the protocol, without any overt move on the part of Her Britannic Majesty's Government.

The protocol consisted of four points: that China should conclude a treaty of amity and commerce with Portugal, as with other European nations; that by this treaty, China should confirm 'the perpetual occupation and government of Macao and its dependencies by Portugal, as any other Portuguese possession'; that Macao should take steps to control the opium trade on lines similar to those being taken at Hongkong; and— the British clause—that Portugal should undertake 'never to alienate Macao and its dependencies without agreement with China'.

The treaty, drawn up shortly afterwards, was signed at Tientsin on 1 December 1887, and ratified the following year. It was a characteristic last touch to British relations with Macao that, even when the Portuguese settlement finally achieved the rights it demanded, it only did so when and because this suited British interests.

The pursuit of sovereign rights was, in fact, the pursuits of an illusion, though it did not seem so in the nineteenth century, when so much of the world was ruled by the European colonial powers, and matters concerning treaties and territorial rights were of greater significance than they are today.

Moreover, the element of duress on China's part introduced into the situation a feature which was untraditional and did not make for cordiality. Though China, imperial and subsequently republican, adhered to the treaty, she did so with scrupulous regard to Macao's exact territorial limits, which were the subject of further disputes. The truth was that although the treaty may have improved Macao's status in respect of other European nations, and Hongkong, it worsened it with China; and the relationship with China was far the more important.

The riposte came in 1966-7, when China's Cultural Revolution overflowed into Macao's streets, with the special local feature that it was aimed at the emblems and symbols of Portuguese sovereignty, as well as at authority in general. The overwhelming nature of the demonstrations showed where sovereignty lies in Macao. The administration was paralyzed, and from then on assumed a more modest posture, in keeping with how it used to be, before the trauma induced by the Treaty of Nanking.

In the aftermath of the Portuguese revolution of 1974, when Portugal divested herself of her colonies, it might have seemed that Macao, most anomalous of all Portuguese possessions, would be the first to have its flag hauled down. An anomaly from the start, however, anomaly at this juncture piled on anomaly. Regardless of Portuguese revolutionary opinion, Lisbon was informed that China wished Macao to remain as it was. Portuguese troops were withdrawn, leaving the city as undefended as it was in its heyday, reverting indeed, in respect of China, to a situation which is an almost exact parallel with how it was at the very beginning.

Finest hour

It remains to pay tribute to the help Macao gave to untold thousands of Hongkong people reduced to destitution and starvation during the Second World War.

Like Hongkong, Macao during this century has had to sustain a succession of what may be described as tidal waves of refugees, driven there by unsettled conditions in China and the Far East. Many Europeans normally residing in China took refuge in Macao during the Boxer rising of 1900, and again between 1922 and 1927, during the anti-foreign movement that marked the rise of the Kuomintang to power in China. An even more serious increase in population took place in 1938 when the Japanese, having invaded China the year before, advanced rapidly southwards and took Canton. This time the bulk of the refugees was Chinese, and the numbers were far greater. The population had not begun to decline before 8 December 1941, when the Japanese invaded Hongkong from the mainland, and captured and occupied it after a seventeen-day battle. This time

135

the refugee problem was to be on an unprecedented scale, and in circumstances far graver than any experienced before.

Although Portugal was neutral in the Second World War, there was a grave danger that Japan would overlook this in respect of Macao, particularly if it sheltered refugees from Hongkong. The Governor, Commander Gabriel Teixeira (1940–6), decided to take this risk, and hospitably opened Macao's doors to all comers. All goods, such as cloth, fuel, and machinery, which the Japanese might be expected to find themselves short of as the war progressed, were requisitioned and gradually released as barter for rice, firewood, and other necessities. The whole of the gambling taxes—$2,000,000—were made over by the government to the assistance of refugees. Indeed, Macao's entire conduct during the period from Christmas 1941 to August 1945, when Hongkong was under Japanese occupation, was a gesture of unselfish friendship, made in Portugal's traditional style, regardless of dangers which others less magnanimous might have thought it more prudent to avoid.

In Hongkong the Japanese interned all members of the British fighting services, including the Hongkong Volunteer Defence Corps, composed of men of many races, and also all British-born civilians. The rest were left to fend for themselves. But with trade at a standstill, a steadily inflating currency, and a shortage of food which by 1944 had culminated in famine conditions in may parts of Kwangtung, nearly the whole of the Eurasian and Portuguese communities were obliged to take refuge in Macao, where the British Consul had funds at his disposal for the relief of families of Hongkong Volunteers and other distressed British subjects. With them came numerous Chinese whose previous associations with the British made a temporary retirement expedient.

With a population swollen to well over half a million, threatened with blockade, and later with occupation, by the

Japanese, and bordered by a province sinking into anarchy and famine, Macao managed to survive a period that certainly ranks as one of the most remarkable in its history. Various groups acted as transmitters of war information, and assisted many on war service to escape through Japanese-controlled territory into Kuomintang China. After the war, with equal goodwill, Macao went out of its way to provide leave and rest centres for the great numbers of Allied troops in the Far East.

The patient endurance of the Macanese during these fateful years, and the sagacity and foresight of their Governor, can hardly be overestimated, while the British Consul, John Pownall Reeves, whose community of refugees, sustaining their morale in times when, to many of them, all seemed lost, won himself a unique place in the city's respect and affection.

No one who experienced Macao's hospitality during these years would ever forget it. The entire episode ranks as one of the city's finest moments.

Where so much is enshrined

Macao is of course a part—a very real part—of the worldwide monument to Portugal's achievement in drawing Europe and Asia closer together, thereby immeasurably improving the well-being of mankind. Yet despite its people's passionate attachment to Portugal, Macao has always lived a life of its own, part of an inter-Asian trading system connected with Europe only at two points' remove. The major Portuguese historians of the past knew so little about it that one finds scarcely a reference to it, while after 1641 it virtually disappears from historical ken.

At that time, everything pointed to the city's loss of identity, and to its mixed-race population slowly melting into the Chinese environment. The miracle is not simply that it survived, but that the people never lost their europeanness. They were in fact guardians of European culture, as became apparent in

137

Hongkong's early days, when had it not been for the Protuguese there would have been no cultural life whatever. Hongkong's first theatre, a masterpiece of elegance, was Portuguese, and throughout the Victorian period nothing could be done in music or drama without drawing on Portuguese talent. When one reflects that these were people who had never been to Europe, they or their forebears stretching back sometimes more than two centuries, this can in a sense be called the true marvel of Macao.

Culturally there has never been anything like Macao, where so much of China and so much of Europe are enshrined in one small place. Goa, for all the magnificence of its buildings, never achieved this. Goa is European; the Indian element is missing. Only in Macao can one experience the extraordinary sensation of being one moment in the Lin Fong Temple, and ten minutes later in the Teatro Dom Pedro V, each an emphatic expression of a disparate civilization, yet producing no sense of cultural clash. Everything of distinction in Macao tones into the mellowness of the place, the whole creating a peculiar cultural unity, which is unique.

Temples in China, if constructed authentically, should have no foundations. The Lin Fong Temple is so designed. It is built on a plate of granite, set upon the surface of the earth without foundations, and is a small masterpiece of temple architecture. Though it is at the other end of the city, near the barrier gate, it is in fact an extension of the original Ma Cho Temple. Founded around 1570, it reached its present proportions in 1872. Its bronze bells date far back into the 1600s, each bell the gift of one or other of the Pearl River districts, in gratitude to the Macao community for building and repairing their ships.

The Teatro Dom Pedro V, were it refurbished, would rank with the Fenice in Venice, and the Manuel in Valletta, as one of the most attractive of all European theatres. The actual *salle*, though it does not appear to be, is in fact a perfect circle, set in a building which is a rectangle. Its cooling arrangements, with its ceiling air vents, are masterly. The *foyer* is about the most perfectly proportioned European room in Asia.

One may turn from there to the memorial home of Dr Sun Yat-sen, founder and first President of the Chinese Republic. For a short time before the Revolution of 1911, to which he devoted his life, he practised medicine in Macao—he was Hongkong's first medical graduate. The collection of photographs of him in the house, showing the speed with which he aged in the agonizing years spent trying to keep China united after the Empire was overthrown, is of itself a most moving document of a man's life.

If one knows a Catholic father, a tour of the seminary of St Joseph gives an idea of the grandeur with which Portuguese built in their small enclave's early days.

Then there is the inescapable, the St Paul's ruin. After the Jesuit Order was closed down, at the end of the eighteenth century, the Jesuit seminary buildings on the slopes of the Monte eventually became a barracks; and in January 1835 these caught fire. A stiff east wind was blowing. The fire was so intense that the flames licked across the intervening space, and caught the church, which was consumed within a few minutes, leaving only the stone façade standing.

Yet in some ways the destruction was an enhancement. The façade on its own, with its eyeless windows, open to the sky atop their magnificent stone flight of ascending steps, is almost more impressive than it must have been when the church was with it, one of the most astonishing architectural moments in all Asia.

Finally comes the Camões Museum, in which Macao and what it represents as regards China comes eloquently to life. The former property of Manuel Pereira, and residence of East

India Company grandees, it is a superb mansion, conveying a vivid sense of how life was in the eighteenth century. Among other things, it contains one of the finest collection of Shekwan statuary, a school of work exclusive to Kwangtung.

The crunch comes when one notices in one of the inner walls an elaborately carved stone tablet inscribed to the earth god, complete with red candles and other appurtenances for worship at suitable times.

How does one sum this up?

The other day, up at the Rocks of Camões, I noticed a Chinese student walking very slowly reading a book, so engrossed in what he was reading that he was unaware he was walking. Passing very slowly beneath the bronze bust of the immortal Camões, he was reading the poems of equally immortal Li Po, the Omar Khayyám of China.

Meanwhile, down there at the casino, twenty-four hours day and night, the wheels were spinning round and round.

Bibliography

A great deal about Macao's early history went unrecorded and is unknown. Portuguese official chroniclers and contemporary historians scarcely refer to it, and it was not until the last 100 years that the past was brought gradually to reveal its secrets, thanks to the work of modern scholars, of whom the most notable are the Marques Pereiras, Montalto de Jesus, J.M. Braga, Professor Charles Boxer, Father Gervaix, Jordão de Freitas, Dr Armando Cortesão, Luis Gonzaga Gomes, and Father Manuel Teixeira. As a result of their efforts, the picture has become, as J.M. Braga put it, 'fairly intelligible'.

Apart from various minor points arising from this author's own investigations, the present work follows these authorities. Any unattributed quotation in the text is from one or other of the works of J.M. Braga, whose magnificent collection of printed works on the Portuguese in the Far Eastis accessible to the public in the National Library of Australia, Canberra.

The following is a select list of works consulted.

C.R. Boxer. *Fidalgos in the Far East*, 1550–1770 (Martinus Nijhoff, The Hague, 1948), reprinted by Oxford University Press in its Oxford in Asia Historical Reprints series.

—*The Christian Century in Japan*, 1549–1650 (University of California Press, 1951).

— *The Great Ship from Amacon*, (1959).

J.M. Braga. *The Western Pioneers and Their Discovery of Macao* (Imprensa Nacional, Macao, 1949).

—*China Landfall*, 1513, Boletim do Instituto Português de Hongkong, No. 4, June 1955.

—*Hongkong and Macao*, Noticias de Macau, 1951, revised edition, 1960.

Luis Vaz de Camoens. *The Lusiads*, translated from Portuguese by William C. Atkinston (Penguin Books, London, 1952).

Suzanne Chantal. *Histoire du Portugal* (Hachette, Paris, 1965).

Austin Coates. *Prelude to Hongkong* (Routledge and Kegan Paul, London, 1966).

Maurice Collis. *The Grand Peregrination* (Faber, London, 1949).

G.R. Crone. *The Discovery of the East* (Hamish Hamilton, London, 1972).

Sir William Foster, C.I.E. *England's Quest of Eastern Trade* (A. and C. Black, London, 1933).

Francisco Luiz Gomes. *Le Marquis de Pombal, esquisse de sa vie publique* (Imprimerie Franco-Portugaise, Lisbon, 1869).

William C. Hunter. *Bits of Old China* (Kelly and Walsh, Shanghai, 1911; first published Kegan Paul, London, 1885).

—*The 'Fan Kwae' at Canton Before Treaty Days*, 1825–1844, The Oriental Affairs, Shanghai, 1938 (first published 1882).

Robin Hutcheon. *Chinnery, The Man and the Legend* (South China Morning Post, Hongkong, 1975).

H.V. Livermore. *A History of Portugal* (Cambridge, 1947).

—*A New History of Portugal* (Cambridge, 1966).

Andrew Ljungstedt. *An Historical Sketch of the Portuguese Settlements in China* (James Munroe, Boston, 1836).

C.A. Montalto de Jesus. *Historic Macao* (Salesian Printing Press, Macao, 1926; first edition 1902).

Robert Morrison, D.D. *Memoirs of*, compiled by his widow (Longman, Orme, Brown, Green, and Longmans, London, 1839).

Peter Mundy. *The Travels of, in Europe and Asia, 1608–1667*, Vol. III, Parts I and II; edited by Lt.-Col. Sir Richard Carnac Temple, Bt., C.B., C.I.E., F.S.A. (Hakluyt Society, London, 1919).

Friar Domingo Navarrete. *The Travels and Controversies of, 1618–1686*, edited from manuscript and printed sources by J.S. Cummins (Hakluyt Society, Cambridge, 1962).

G.B. Sansom. *The Western World and Japan* (The Cresset Press, London, 1950).

G.R. Sayer. *Hong Kong, Birth, Adolescence, and Coming of Age* (Oxford, 1937).

Portuguese Manuel Teixeira. *A Gruta de Camões em Macao* (Imprensa Nacional, Macao, 1977).

Index

Aberdeen, Lord, Foreign Secretary, 115

Adams, Will, pilot and shipwright, 66

Albuquerque, Afonso de, Viceroy, 6, 7, 8

Alexander VI, Pope, 15

Almeida, Francisco de, Viceroy, 5, 6

Alvares, Jorge, 7, 8–10

Amaral, Capt. João Maria Ferreira do, 116–19, 120–21, 122–23, 124, 127

Andrade, Simão Peres de, 13

Arriaga, Miguel de, 87–91, 92–4, 95, 98

Beale, Thomas, 87–91

Beresford, Lord, 91

Best, Capt. Thomas, 64

Bocarro, Manuel, gunsmith, 57

Bonham, Sir George, Governor of Hongkong 119, 120, 123

Bowring, Sir John, Governor of Hongkong, 103, 129

Bremer, Commodore Sir James John Gordon, 110

Bruce, Frederick, 130–31

Camões, Luis Vaz de, 33–5, 53, 79–80, 84, 103, 104, 139–40

Carmichael, William, 63–5

Castilho, João de architect, 79, 80

Castro Cabral, Governor, 92–4, 101

Cataneo, Father, S.J., 56

Chang Tê Emperor, 11, 12

Charles I of England, 69

Ch'ia Ching Emperor, 12, 22

Chinnery, George, artist, 108–9

Chü Yuan, Governor of Fukien, 20, 21, 22

Coelho do Amaral, José Rodrigues, Governor, 128, 132

Cunha, Pedro Alexandrino da, Governor, 128

Cushing, Caleb, U.S. Minister to China, 112–13

D'Aguilar, Maj.-Gen. G.C., 116

Davis, Sir John Francis, Governor of Hongkong, 116–17, 119

Davis, John W., U.S. Commissioner, 123

Dias, Bartolomeu, 3

Elgin, Earl of, 130–31

Elizabeth I of England, 54, 55

Elliot, Capt. Charles, R.N., 106, 110

Ferreira do Amaral, see Amaral

Forth-Rouen, Baron, 123

Frobisher, Joan, 66–7

Frobisher, Richard, ship carpenter, 66–7

Fukien community, in Macao, 36–7, 52

Gama, Vasco da, 3, 14, 34, 79–80
Gonçalves Cardoso, Governor 128
Gros, Baron, 130–31
Guimarães, Capt. Isidoro Francisco, 128–29, 130–31

Hart, Sir Robert, 133
Henrique, Cardinal-king, 53, 80
Henry the Navigator, Prince, 1, 3
Hideyoshi, shogun, 47–8, 73
Hsü Kuang-tsin, Governor of Kwangtung, 119, 120, 127
Hung Hsiu-ch'uan, 130

Jehangir, Mughal Emperor, 55
João I, King of Portugal, 1
João II, 67
João III, 15, 72, 80
João IV, 76–78
João V, 84–5
João VI, as Prince Regent 86, as King 91–2
José I, 85
Judith, or Julia, 66–8
Junot, Marshal, Duc d'Abrantes, 87

Keppel, Admiral Sir Henry, 121–22
Kiying, Imperial Plenipotentiary, 113–14, 116–18, 119

Lagrené, Théodose de, 113
Leonor, Queen, 67
Lin Fu, Governor of Kwangtung, 21
Lin Tse-hsü, Imperial High Commissioner, 105–6, 107, 122
Linschoten, Jan Huyghen van, 54
Ljungstedt, Andrew, 110, 111–12
Lobo da Silveira, Sebastião, Capt.-Gen., 77

Mactan, Raja of, 16
Magellan, 13, 16, 53
Manuel I, King of Portugal, 14, 15, 72, 80
Maria I, Queen of Portugal, 86
Maria II, 118
Marques, Commendador Lourenço, 103
Mas, Sinibaldo de, 123
Mascarenhas, Francsisco, Capt.-Gen., 61
Melo Coutinho, Martim Afonso de 13
Mendes Pinto, Fernão, 19–20, 27, 28, 33
Mesquita, Col. Vicente Nicolau de, 123, 124–5
Methwold, William, 70
Miguel, Prince 95
Morrison, Mary, 99
Morrison, Dr. Robert, 99–100
Mundy, Peter, 41, 46, 68, 69, 75

Navarrete, Friar Domingo, 81
Noronha, Miguel de, Viceroy, 70

Palmerston, Lord, 110, 122
Pegado, José Gregorio, Governor, 116
Pereira, Manuel, Privy Councillor, 101, 102, 139
Perestrello, Raffaelo, 10, 63
Pires, Tomé, 10–13, 17, 18, 24
Philip II of Spain, 53–4, 63
Philip III, 55
Philip IV, 69
Philippa of Lancaster, 1
Pinheiro, Bordalo, sculptor, 103
Pombal, Marquês de, 85

Pottinger, Sir Henry, Governor of
    Hongkong, 110

Reeves, John Pownall, 137
Reijersen, Cornelis van, 57–8
Rho, Father, S.J., 59

São João de Porto Alegre, BAron,
    88, 98
Sebastião, King of Portugal, 53, 80
Silveira Pinto, Adrião Accacio de,
    Governor, 104–5, 106–7
Skellater, John Forbes, 86
Smith, Capt., R.N., 107
Sousa, Leonel de, 25, 32
Summers, James, teacher, 120, 121
Sun Yat-sen, 139

Tao Kuang Emperor, 105
Teixeira, Commander Gabriel,
    Governor, 136
Tokugawa Iemitsu, shogun, 73–5
Tokugawa Ieyasu, shogun, 73
Tyler, John, Pres. of U.S., 112

Vieira, Tomas, 61
Villalobos, Ruy Lopez de, 32

Weddell, Capt., John, 75–6
Wellesley, Marquess, 111

Xavier, St Francis, 22, 24–5, 44

Yu Tai-yau, 29
Yung Lo Emperor, 12, 17